CONCILIUM

CONCILIUM 2006/3

WOMEN'S VOICES IN WORLD RELIGIONS

Edited by
Hille Haker, Susan Ross and
Marie-Theres Wacker

SCM Press · London

Published by SCM Press, 9–17 St Albans Place, London N1 0NX

ISBN 0 334 03089 7

Printed and bound in Great Britain by
William Clowes Ltd, Beccles, Suffolk

Concilium Published February, April, June, October
December

Contents

Introduction:
Women's Voices in World Religions

HILLE HAKER, SUSAN ROSS AND MARIE-THERES WACKER

With the beginning of the new millennium, we observe a new political concern for women's concerns – be it in the Millennium Goals of the United Nations, or the World Development Reports that critically analyse the milestones that have been reached – and those that were forgotten in favour of other issues on the political agenda in international politics. On the other hand, we also observe a renewed conservatism in all world religions and within the study of religion, which we need to address.

In this issue, we take a look at the actual situation of women in different religions – as seen by those actors who in their particular cultural and religious traditions try to find their own perspectives, institutional positions and a space to reflect upon what it means for women to address their own questions. We hope to offer some insight into what women in different religions consider important, where they stand today; in this we wish to create some space for further interaction and dialogue. This we consider the most important outcome of this methodologically rather unusual issue. There have always been feminist theological contributions to specific issues of *Concilium*, as well as several issues that have been dedicated specifically to feminist theology. In contrast, this issue reflects on women's actual situations in their specific contexts.

We decided to ask women themselves to share their experiences and views. We asked them to write about their understanding and experiences of being a woman in their particular tradition and what they consider to be central questions today; to write about the institutional structures and the organization of leadership, and to focus on women's participation in leadership. Furthermore, we wanted to know the state of affairs of women's studies/feminism/gender theory in their traditions, and whether this approach is helpful for their own work, whether it is established on an institutional level. However, we did not send out a questionnaire or make use of any kind of sociological methodology, but rather sought to hear the authors' own voices into speech.

While we were waiting for and reading the first articles, we began a conversation among ourselves about our own traditions, being European and Northern American editors, rather arbitrarily focusing on our own situation. The result of this beginning conversation is documented in our own contribution, as our own personal accounts, together with some initial information on feminism in Catholicism and Protestantism.

With inter-religious dialogue becoming more and more important in our social as well as in our academic contexts, we hope to provide you with texts written by those who are rarely asked first to contribute to the endeavour of inter-religious dialogue. With our more or less autobiographical approach, we believe that it is possible to intensify our own dialogue, and raise those questions which are of pivotal importance for us.

In the first section, two *Jewish* scholars give their account. *Adele Reinhartz* begins with a question that perhaps every religious person needs to address: the question of identity. With respect to women's role and women's identity within Judaism, she distinguishes between participation in the community life of a particular synagogue and identification within one of the Jewish denominations or movements. With regard to women's roles in the synagogue, she distinguishes between lay and cultic functions, on the one hand, and the different denominations, on the other. She also describes the diversity within Judaism: there are Orthodox, Conservative, Reform, Reconstructionist and Havurah movements, each of which has rather different perspectives on the role of women. Reinhartz's personal account is the way of a Jewish woman and mother who holds the Jewish way of life in high esteem but who, at the same time, subscribes to egalitarian, that is, feminist views. Reinhartz shows how she faces this tension, and concludes that in her own thinking it was not so much feminist theory but the practical women's movement that has most influenced her.

Elisa Klapheck, rabbi in Amsterdam, the Netherlands, gave us an interview in which she takes up our questions, and gives some insight into her work and position in the *Beit Ha'Chidush*. She talks about the transition from being an 'ordinary' member of the community to holding a position of responsibility and gives her own account of how she was encouraged by Jewish feminist scholars. In the last part of the interview, Klapheck turns to the present situation of Jewish women in positions of leadership (such as rabbis, cantors, academics) and argues for a distinct European Jewish identity.

In the section on *Christianity*, *Anne Nasimiyu-Wasike* writes about the status of women in traditional family structures in Kenya, and gives her own account of how Christianity on the one hand played into the hands of the existing patriarchal structures that considered women subordinate, but also extended this devaluation in considering them inappropriate for ritual services and positions of leadership, contrary to the roles women play in traditional African religion. Nasimiyu-Wasike addresses the problems of the difficult social and economic situation, and sheds light on its effects, particularly on women and girls. Although gender studies and feminism have been introduced in academic life in Kenya, it becomes clear that Christianity in Africa still has a long way to go before women's potential is acknowledged and developed.

Katerina Karkala-Zorba introduces the Orthodox perspective, focusing on women's roles in the Orthodox Church and in religious life. Drawing on Paul's concept of unity in Christ, she holds that the question of gender is a secondary question for Orthodox Christians. There is, however, a rich tradition and a place for women within the hierarchy that Karkala-Zorba interprets affirmatively. She criticizes feminist theology from a western point of view for not leaving sufficient room for a constructive interpretation of the tradition. At present, the ordination of women as deaconesses is being discussed within Orthodoxy, although the question of marriage raises other issues.

Virginia R. Azcuy, writing from an Argentinian background, emphasizes the roots of the Christian feminist movement in the tradition of liberation theology, but also stresses the critical relationship within that tradition because of its underlying understanding of femininity and gender roles. Women in general and female theologians in particular face a difficult situation in Latin America: although academia is open to them by now in most of the countries, the prospects of a professional life are rather dim. For this reason, women have begun to develop networks at the university level as well as at the level of pastoral work. This, she holds, is the first step in developing a distinctive perspective for feminist theology.

In the section on *Islam, Hamideh Mohagheghi* writes from her perspective as an Iranian-born Muslim woman living in Germany. She analyses women's scholarship and women's role in the teaching and interpretation of the Qur'an throughout history, and addresses the difficulty in the relationship of feminist theory and women's religious lives. Furthermore, she sees the tensions of German Muslim women who are caught in the challenge of adaptation to western culture while maintaining their own identity. Though arguing that both do not contradict each other, Mohagheghi is as critical of some western developments in lifestyle and culture as she is critical of some interpretations of the Muslim tradition. But she emphasizes that there is a specific Muslim 'enlightenment' tradition that women (and men) in Islam can make use of today.

Mehrézia Labidi-Maïza gives a personal account of her upbringing in Northern Africa and her decision to live women's emancipation without neglecting her religious tradition. The *hijab*, for her first and foremost a spiritual expression, has become a political symbol of Muslim women's struggle to find their own identity and position. Labidi-Maïza shows how she has come to learn to acknowledge the religious and cultural differences between herself, a highly educated Northern African woman with French nationality, and other Muslim women in her life context. She concludes by confirming equity and equality among men and women, which is needed to realize the partnership and solidarity upon which Islam is based.

In the section on *Hinduism, Madhu Khanna*'s article presents a thorough and rich survey of the history of women's role in the Indian Hindu tradition, from the high valuation of the ancient goddesses, the increasing claim to women's subordination because of their inborn evil nature, to the 'modern' struggle for equality and female identity since the nineteenth century. Khanna explores the gap between urban (élite) empowering and (rural) gender inequality; women's participation in local politics, and the question of leadership within the Hindu tradition. Moreover, she introduces new initiatives in feminist and gender studies, together with the establishment of centres for women's studies, and argues for a hermeneutics that could enrich the feminist approach which at present has a rather 'western' shape. In order to address the Indian and Hindu diversity and plurality, she develops a framework for gender research, starting with critical text analysis, the exploration of the Goddess tradition, and the regional oral sources representing the diverse Hindu culture and religion.

Lina Gupta offers more insight into one specific part of the Hindu tradition, namely the Autumn Festival of the goddesses in India. Brought up in India as a Hindu, Gupta came to share the ecofeminist approach in the USA, and did a lot of research on the Hindu Goddess tradition. In her article, she draws not only on this but also integrates the voices of Indian Hindu women she interviewed during several trips to India; often enough, she claims, Hindu women are met with western prejudices about their actual lives, so that spreading their views in itself can be seen as critiquing particular western victimizing attitudes towards Hindu women. Describing the Autumn Festival of the goddesses, as it is celebrated in Bengal, Gupta responds to the assumed equation of Hindu women and oppression, and gives a lively picture of the 'source of strength and power of Hindu women'. Centred around the 'mother goddess' Durga, women find a space to interrupt their ordinary lives where inequality is more caste-based than gender-based, as one of the interviewed women, Maya Sen, writes. In the final part of her article, Gupta focuses on the major concepts of Hinduism that have influenced her, namely the concept of the divine, of self-realization, of respect for other traditions, and of active non-violence.

In the section on *Buddhism*, *Young-Mi Kim* reflects upon the Korean Buddhist tradition that has had a very important impact on Korean history especially between 918 and 1392. Neo-Confucianism, she recalls, brought an end to women's admission to temples, and their subordination and confinement to the family circle remained more or less unchanged until the twentieth century. With regard to Buddhism, however, she notes that even in the times of Buddhist oppression by Neo-Confucianism, women did not comply as well as men did with the restrictions – resulting in the fact that women are now the vast majority of Buddhist believers, as well as in the religious orders. Kim tells how a woman's religious life is centred on the family, without her having much opportunity to participate in public social and political life. Furthermore, she also sheds light on the life of Buddhist nuns. The last decades, Kim writes, have seen a shift in the attention to social as well as gender issues in Korean society and within Buddhism – due mostly to lay women and nuns who made this shift possible. Kim explores the Buddhist tradition with respect to gender equality, and shows how different schools present different views on this. Despite this, the Korean Buddhist Women's Development Institute was established in the late 1980s, and has taken up several social projects together with inter-religious collaboration with the Christian Church.

Rita Gross, US-Buddhist feminist scholar, writes about her long journey into Buddhism, particularly as a western feminist who could not and would not close her eyes to the tensions between this religion and feminism. Looking back at her own personal experiences, it becomes clear that feminism in Buddhism for her is first and foremost a question of spiritual leadership. Gross argues that as long as there is no equality in this leadership, namely as many female teachers of Buddhism as male teachers, she cannot see that gender does not matter. Writing about her relationships to both male and female teachers, she emphasizes this claim that connects the two main sources of her religious identity: feminist Buddhism.

This issue ends with a bibliography on 'Women in World Religions' that we hope will be helpful for anybody who wants to continue her or his reading.

I. Judaism

Women in Judaism

ADELE REINHARTZ

Thinking about the question of the role of women in Judaism, it is most often the roles of women in the synagogue or in Jewish religious practice, liturgy and institutions that come to mind. This is not inappropriate, as it is in the realm of religion that the role of women has changed the most over the past several decades and which currently still poses challenges for many of us who are deeply involved in Jewish communal life.

Yet it is important to understand that Judaism encompasses far more than the synagogue, religious practice or liturgy, and that to reduce it to being a 'religion' is to misunderstand the scope of the label, the nature of Jewish identity and the experience and the roles of women in Judaism.

This was brought home to me rather forcefully during my first week as an undergraduate student at the University of Toronto. Coming from a strongly committed but secular Jewish background, I had decided that it was time to learn more about Judaism and enrolled in a course entitled simply 'Introduction to Judaism'. The professor began the very first class by asking his students to define Judaism. Various people had immediate answers: Judaism is 'a religion', 'a race', 'a culture'. Yet for each answer, there immediately arose a problem. If Judaism is a religion, then how do we take into account the thousands of Jews who are non-practising, agnostic or even atheistic and yet continue to define themselves as Jewish? If Judaism is a race, which, for example, was how it was considered during the Nazi regime, then how do we make room in this definition for those who were not born into Judaism but have chosen to convert? If Judaism is a culture, then which culture is it? There are Jews all over the world, and they have developed an extraordinary variety of cultures, from the Yiddish-speaking heritage of Eastern European Judaism and the Arabic-speaking heritage of Jews in North Africa and Arabia to the Jews of Ethiopia who speak Amharic, but also

Ge'ez and Tigrinya. The conclusion our class came to was that it was not possible to limit Judaism to any of these factors. Jews are a people, not a religion, a race or a culture. There is a minimal, technical definition: being Jewish means either being born of a Jewish mother or joining Judaism through a formal process of conversion. However, being Jewish also means having a sense of identity, a sense of belonging to a particular people that has gone through particular historical pathways, whether one has been born into that people or travelled along those pathways oneself.

To be a Jewish woman means to be part of this worldwide and diverse community. It means that one's sense of identification and belonging can be expressed in countless ways. One can aspire to certain values that are Jewish, one can be absorbed with Jewish history including the Holocaust; one can participate in Jewish communal organizations, singing groups, formal or informal classes on aspects of Judaism, book clubs, cooking classes; one can visit Israel, learn Hebrew or Yiddish, and engage in a myriad of other activities all of which both foster and also reflect Jewish identification. For many Jewish women, including myself, being Jewish also entails participating actively at a local level in a small number of overlapping spheres, for the benefit of others, and for the satisfaction, enjoyment and richness that such participation brings to my own life.

The concept of role of women in Judaism can also refer to women's roles in the synagogue. Here, however, a number of distinctions must be made.

First, it is important to note that Jewish identity, that is, a person's specific understanding of and position on the role of women and many other issues, is not necessarily tied in any way to the type of synagogue that person chooses to attend or where they pay their dues. In my own case, while I attend and currently pay membership dues at an Orthodox synagogue, I do not identify myself as Orthodox. And I am by no means unique in this regard. While it would be more unusual for Jews who identify themselves as Orthodox to attend non-Orthodox synagogues, in many Canadian cities there may well be a majority of people attending an Orthodox synagogue on a given Sabbath who do not formally identify themselves as Orthodox and do not necessarily adhere to other aspects of an Orthodox lifestyle.

Second, one should distinguish between women's role in the lay leadership of synagogues, including participation on the Board of Directors. This type of participation is increasingly open to women, including top leadership roles such as President. A more complicated matter is that of women's participation in the ritual aspects of the worship service.

Third, in considering women's roles in the synagogue one must distinguish among various streams or denominations, since the role of women varies considerably from one stream to another. Even within these streams there are many options, due to the absence of a centralized authority that would impose uniformity on individual congregations.

In any synagogue service, women's access to participation may vary from one component of the service to another. In most formal synagogues, there is a rabbi who presides over the service. The rabbi may or may not lead one or more parts of the service; he or she may do a sermon, or lead a class or study session during or after the service. It is important to note, however, that the presence of a rabbi is not essential for a full religious service to take place. In contrast to Roman Catholicism, for example, there is no special liturgical function which can only be done by a rabbi, whether at a regular Sabbath service or on special festivals. The service may be entirely led by lay people, as long as they have the knowledge required.

The main components of the Saturday morning service, the high point of the weekly liturgical calendar, are the chanting of the liturgy, the reading of the weekly portion from the Torah (the Pentateuch or the Five Books of Moses) and the chanting of the Haftarah, which is a supplementary reading from the prophetic literature that follows after the Torah portion has been read. Before and after the 'Torah service' (reading of Torah and Haftarah), the Torah scroll is paraded around the room so that is can be touched or kissed by the congregants. There are also 'honours' consisting of reciting of blessings before and after each segment of the Torah reading, as well as before and after the Haftarah. In most cases, the person receiving the honours of reciting the Torah blessings will not him- or herself be doing the actual chanting, as considerable knowledge is required that many congregants do not have. By contrast, the person who is chanting the Haftarah will also have the 'honour' of reciting the blessings before and after that reading.

The most rigid policies around women's participation occur within Orthodox congregations, though these may vary from excluding women almost entirely from the proceedings to including them as much as possible within particular limits. In Orthodox congregations women and men sit in separate sections of the synagogue. Often there is a curtain or other barrier separating men and women, and in many circles this barrier needs to be high enough so that there can be no eye contact between the two groups. The reason for this separation is to avoid distraction if at all possible. The services are conducted from the men's side and the Torah is read from that side as well. In some congregations, including my own, the Torah is paraded close to the women's section so that women can also touch or kiss it before and after the Torah service. Exclusion from active participation in the service is a problematic issue for many women, including myself, but in fairness it must be said that many Orthodox women are not uncomfortable with this situation and enjoy the opportunity to sit among other women during the service, and use the time not only for prayer but for contemplation and quiet respite from the pressures of everyday life.

While the non-participation of women within Orthodox worship has remained stable in most circles, there are signs of change that also signal the impact of feminist activism. One obvious area is Jewish education. More and more institutions are offering education in the traditionally male domain of Jewish law and rabbinic literature (Mishnah and Talmud, the foundational Jewish legal texts) in response to women's demands. And in a small number of congregations, notably in Jerusalem but also elsewhere, there are Orthodox congregations that are opening up as widely as they can within an Orthodox framework to allow for women's participation. One notable example is the congregation Shirah Hadashah ('New Song') in Jerusalem. Although men and women sit separately, and there is a rather high curtain that separates them, women receive Torah honours, chant the Haftarah and lead certain parts of the service. This is a revolutionary landmark within Orthodox Judaism and has provided a role model for others who are concerned about women's roles but wish to remain within an Orthodox framework.

In North America, in Israel and, gradually, in other parts of the world, the Conservative movement ('Masorti' in Israel) has been an important force with regard to Jewish worship. The Conservative movement, like Orthodoxy, accepts the importance of Jewish law as a divinely ordained way of life but it explicitly views *halakhah* as dynamic and thus open to modification according to certain well-defined criteria. Many view the fact of mixed seating as the outstanding difference between Orthodoxy and Conservative Judaism, but in fact the differences extend much more deeply than this.

The Conservative movement as a whole has been ordaining women for about thirty years, and there are numerous women in the rabbinical seminaries that prepare rabbis for the Conservative movement. In Canada there are as yet few women rabbis, as Canada tends to lag behind the USA in making these changes. But there are some and numbers are likely to grow. Many synagogues have made changes in the last ten to twenty years which provide opportunities for women to participate in the service. These range from allowing women to have Torah honours, to permitting them to chant the Torah and Haftarah. A handful are fully egalitarian, among them the Beth Jacob synagogue in Hamilton, with which I and my family were affiliated for many years.

In Reform Judaism women have long been trained to be rabbis, and have had full participation in the synagogue services. Reform does not adhere to the traditional *halakhah* in a strict way, and initially it even rejected many aspects of it, including the dietary laws and many of the laws that circumscribe activities on the Sabbath such as driving and working. But in recent years many Reform rabbis have adopted more traditional modes of behaviour and this sometimes extends to synagogues themselves. The situation is similar with regard to Reconstructionism, which was an offshoot of Conservative Judaism originally but has gone its way in many different areas. As in the Reform movement, women have been full participants, as ordained rabbis and leaders of all areas of the service, for many decades.

Finally, we turn to Havurah Judaism. The term *havurah* (plural: *havurot*) means simply a group, usually a group much smaller and less formal than a congregation. Some synagogues in fact have *havurot* within them, meaning groups of people who get together regularly for the purposes of worship, study or discussion. Other *havurot* are not affiliated in any way with an institution and consist of people who get together on a weekly, fortnightly or monthly basis, or less frequently, for a variety of purposes related to Jewish worship, Jewish ideas or Jewish life more generally. In North America there is a loose organization of *havurot* called the National Havurah Committee that runs an annual Summer Institute, which is attended by several hundred adults and children. The Institute provides rich opportunities for study, for worship and for enjoyment, in an open, egalitarian and diverse environment. The Institute has been formative in the lives of many Jews who are otherwise unaffiliated, but it also draws individuals and rabbis and other leaders from the Conservative, Reform and Reconstructionist movements. The Institute, and *havurah* movement more generally, has been an important influence in our lives and in the lives of our children.

The variety of forms of religious Judaism, and the larger complex of 'Judaism' that everyone who is Jewish draws on to form their own Jewish identity, makes it very difficult to provide a simple and straightforward answer to the question of what it means to me to be a woman in my tradition.

Perhaps the primary satisfaction that I have experienced in the religious sphere has been the opportunity to acquire the skills of chanting the Haftarah and the Torah, and of leading services in a professional and knowledgeable way. This acquisition has been a long process, which began in 1979 when I was a graduate student in Jerusalem. It was at that time that I started to attend synagogue for the first time in my life and to experience the rhythms of Jewish life, particularly the Sabbath. The synagogue I attended was a Reconstructionist congregation, which I chose precisely because it was fully egalitarian in terms of the roles of men and women. One of the leaders of that congregation ran a seminar in his home to teach women how to read the Haftarah, and it was there that I acquired this skill. Later my husband, who was a professional Torah reader, taught me how to do so and how to lead services. These are skills I have had many opportunities to put to good use. The ability to perform these functions gives one a feeling of mastery of the tradition, and also allows one to contribute particularly to smaller groups where few people might have such skills. Related to this is the importance of raising one's daughters to understand the importance of participation and to provide opportunities for them to acquire the same set of skills, and to raise sons that appreciate and will do what they can to facilitate the education and participation of women within the various Jewish contexts in which they are involved.

Another area of satisfaction has been my participation in a small but active *havurah* in Hamilton, Ontario, which was our home for eighteen years. This *havurah* met monthly in the chapel at a Jewish home for the aged, and the residents in that home were always invited to join us. A number of them took up that invitation on a regular basis, and at our *havurah* several of these elderly women received Torah honours for the first time in their lives. This was an extremely moving and joyful experience not only for them, but also for us.

The central question for me in my current context concerns whether it is possible to move Orthodoxy along to a point of more significant inclusion of women in the worship service. In other movements the situation is either one of full egalitarianism or else a movement towards that goal. In Orthodoxy, however, there is still much work to be done. The development of groups such as Shirah Hadashah is a step in the right direction but even here women are still limited in what they can do. Nor are there possibilities for women to pursue Orthodox rabbinical ordination, although there are one or two small steps being taken by a handful of courageous men and women in that direction as well.

An outsider to the Jewish community might wonder why someone who is committed to feminism and egalitarianism would worship in an Orthodox synagogue or strive for change within Orthodoxy. Given that there are so many options within Judaism that do allow for full and unobstructed participation of women, why not simply gravitate towards those other possibilities? This is of course a feasible course of action, one that many women take and one that I myself followed for many years.

The problem, however, has to do with the fact that the role of women is not an issue that remains isolated from other aspects of Jewish life. Another important aspect has to do with community and lifestyle and specifically the question of Sabbath observance. Traditional Sabbath observance entails not only synagogue worship but also ritual meals, and the abstention from work, driving, writing, cooking and other activities that we engage in throughout the week. In practical terms, Sabbath observance also entails living in proximity to the synagogue and to other people who observe a similar lifestyle. Living within such a community is simply wonderful from a social point of view, and allows the Sabbath truly to be a day that is different from the rest of the week.

The problem lies in the fact that in many areas in North America the Sabbath is often not observed by many people outside of the Orthodox community. Exceptions exist in some major American cities such as New York, Boston, Washington and Philadelphia, but rarely outside of those areas. To be Sabbath observant in a Conservative, Reform or Reconstructionist synagogue can feel rather lonely once one has left the synagogue premises after services.

Due to the perceived conflict between feminist and Orthodox lifestyles, these two options are often mutually exclusive. Thus there is often an uncomfortable and unfortunate choice to be made between belonging to a community in which women have equal opportunity, or to one in which there are other Sabbath-observant families. On the other hand, if one chooses a synagogue for the sake of having a Sabbath community one is almost always foregoing the opportunities for women, which can be very difficult.

Feminist theory and conversation with feminist theologians, critics and theorists both within and outside of my own field of biblical studies have been very helpful not only to my academic work but also to my personal development. Such contacts have helped me to challenge my own presuppositions, encourage my own activism and provide a source of community and support in the struggles that we face in common. Feminist theory in and of itself has in my view had less of an impact on Judaism than has feminist praxis and the feminist movement as a whole. Women have argued for and then received broader opportunities in the secular world, in the world of education and the professions. Jewish women have also sought more participation in their religious lives as well. The impact is evident not only in the fact that most Jewish movements now ordain women rabbis but also in the move towards better Jewish education for girls that spans all movements.

As a Jewish mother, I am optimistic about the opportunities available for our daughters and also for our sons within the variety of Jewish contexts in which they may find themselves throughout their lives. May our efforts, their efforts and those of all women and men continue to bear fruit for the benefit of us all.

'House of Renewal' – A New Form of Judaism

AN INTERVIEW WITH RABBI ELISA KLAPHECK

In May 2005 Elisa Klapheck went as Rabbi to the Beit Ha'Chidush in Amsterdam. The name 'Beit Ha'Chidush' ('House of Renewal') is programmatic for what is still a very young Jewish congregation that places itself in the context of a movement of renewal within contemporary Judaism and explores new ways and horizons on the basis of their own existing tradition. Both of these are important here. One connects with the tradition, more precisely the diversity of Jewish traditions within Orthodoxy as well as Jewish mysticism (Chassidism, Kabbalah), the ethical concepts of Reform Judaism, the Haskala (the Jewish Enlightenment) as well as the movement of 'reconstructionism',[1] with the aim of giving meaning to these traditions in daily life. At the same time there is great openness towards new developments, particularly with regard to the diversity of life forms of men and women who are regarded as equal.

Elisa Klapheck trained as a rabbi by distance learning on a course provided by Aleph, the Alliance for Jewish Renewal.[2] In a combination of residential periods, distance learning, conference telephone conversations, individual training courses and primarily Jewish activities and private study, those with prior knowledge in Judaism are helped to develop a programme of study. For the duration of their studies they are provided with a number of male and female mentors and are able to prepare intellectually and spiritually for their ministry as rabbis. The leadership council of the new community then invited Elisa Klapheck to Amsterdam.

Frau Klapheck, you were one of the co-founders of the egalitarian synagogue in the Oranienburger Straße in Berlin. You also helped make known the story of the first female rabbi in Germany, Regina Jonas, through publishing her dissertation (1930).[3] What did the step of becoming a rabbi yourself mean for you? A dream come true? A goal you achieved? Or something that you had not really planned to do, rather something that 'happened'? Or how would you describe it?
It was a step into responsibility. Prior to it I was very involved, and very much enjoyed it, but I was only involved in areas in which I myself was

interested. The decision to become a rabbi for me was connected with the question about whether I would be able to share the responsibility for the whole, whether I would be able to carry the whole. For example, I enjoyed preaching little occasional homilies in the synagogue and sometimes came out with interpretations quite different from the official readings; I enjoyed involving people in discussions, and it was always important to me that one should have one's own view. The question I had to ask myself was: can I still do that as a rabbi? Was not what mattered in the first instance whether I could submit to the Jewish tradition in its entirety; ought I as a rabbi not first of all to enter into this tradition as a whole – and would I not then also be its representative? Or even more fundamentally: I had to work out my own position with regard to the religion. Within Judaism there is the *halakhah*, the laws – do I practise all of them or only a part, how do I relate these to each other and how do I do this responsibly? And what about God and God's justice? As Jews we have not had that much experience of justice . . . How do we deal with evil in contemporary society, with the many negative experiences in the history of Judaism, and how can one still assent to the basic statements of Jewish monotheism?

The decision to become a rabbi was for me a step into responsibility. And now it goes on: I have the title and people see me as such, probably they also watch me a bit. However, I have noticed that the first ordination is followed by other ordinations. The first one is basically only a blessing from the rabbis, it is only a beginning. The next question is whether the people also ordain you, whether they recognize you as a rabbi. This is where I am at the moment. However, my idea of a rabbi is not a woman leading from the front who tells others what to think. I rather see myself as someone who communicates enough Jewish knowledge to people that they can decide for themselves, so that everyone could be his or her own rabbi. I want to walk with the people and try to explore their potential. As a companion I want to share with them as much of the Jewish tradition as possible, so that on that basis they can develop their own potential and become altogether strong personalities.

What does it mean for you in your religion to be a woman? What are the positive elements which are important to you, and what the obstacles which you as a woman encounter or have encountered?
In my congregation there are no obstacles for me as a woman because it is a congregation which is based from the start on the equality of women. That also applies to the groups in which I have always been involved, in Berlin or in Frankfurt. However, I had to struggle with another obstacle. For a long

time I was afraid to admit that I would play a part in structures of power –
this is a typical female problem, 'psycho-chemical' so to say. However,
confidence is something one can learn. Yes, one has to learn it, every woman
has to come clean in this area, has to admit to her ambitions and work on
herself. It is not the case that men are always to blame when one does not
succeed in some area or other. It is also to do with oneself, and it is important
to be precise and honest with oneself and to analyse one's own weaknesses.

Judaism is a religion of emancipation, starting from the exodus from
slavery to freedom. It is always the small nation, the underdog of a nation,
that is still somehow involved at the top. There is a basic emancipatory
tendency within Judaism which offers me as a woman the possibility to work
for my own emancipation. Women in Judaism are not weak. The opposite is
the case. I would say that this is part and parcel of the religion itself.
However, women did have to work for their place in the synagogue. Such
transgressions of roles can be frightening. One is afraid to destroy Judaism,
if the images no longer match, if there is no longer a man with the Tallit, the
prayer shawl, at the front, but a woman. For me, voices were always important: the singing in the synagogue was always connected with the base voice
of the male cantor. I used to be unable to imagine a female voice on the *bima*.
The sentence from the Talmud that a woman's voice is 'shame' was also alive
in me, and I had to exorcise it from within myself. Today I sing large parts
of the liturgy in the service and with my own voice I contradict this.

Of great importance for me was Regina Jonas, whose work discusses the
question whether women can become rabbis. For this she ploughed through
the entire corpus of rabbinic literature and came to an affirmative conclusion. This has been profoundly motivating for me, as was Jewish feminist
theology with its re-reading of the Bible and of the Talmud, for example
Judith Plaskow's *Standing Again at Sinai* or Susannah Heschel, *On Being a
Jewish Feminist*, but also Pnina Nave Levinson's *Eva und ihre Schwestern*.[4]
These I devoured at the time, and they broadened my own horizon. But now
I have moved on from there. These days I try again to have critical conversations with men; I am now interested in male responses to feminist
challenges.

*Do you already see Jewish men responding or reacting to the questions and posi-
tions of Jewish feminists?*
One example is the issue of circumcision. For me my engagement with
Jewish feminist theology has resulted in beginning to assess circumcision in
a different way. The circumcision of boys, understood as a symbol of the
circumcision of the heart, is against arrogance and the macho-culture. By

now there are also critical voices among Jewish men who can agree with this. In this context I want to mention first of all Daniel Boyarin who describes himself as a Jewish feminist.[5]

Another good example is the *mikwa*, the ritual bath of immersion. In Berlin we once held a workshop on the subject, women and men together. The *mikwa* is normally used by women after their menstruation; men rarely go into the *mikwa* or not at all.[6] We wanted to experience ourselves what the *mikwa* is and what it is like for our whole bodies to be immersed in 'living water'. First we gathered information: I explained the meaning of the *mikwa*, and we discussed it. Then we went into the *mikwa* separately, and later we met again and shared our experiences. Even the men experienced the ritual immersion as a sanctification of the body – as a profound experience.

Within the renewal movement to which I belong this is already general discourse: men reflect on male embodiment, masculinity, authority, the role of the father, about sexuality, the female eros in the male, the male eros in the female, of course also generally about gender issues . . . obviuosly much goes on in the USA, but I would argue that my congregation too has taken up such questions. For them feminism is one of the foundations which they take for granted.

What are the challenges which you see for your congregation within the spectrum of Judaism in the Netherlands?
A number of cities in the Netherlands have Orthodox but also liberal congregations. In Amsterdam there are about twelve thousand Jews; the majority of them, as far as I know, are not part of a congregation.[7] In terms of numbers, the Orthodox congregation is the largest. We are new, a small group, people with very different life stories who share a vision of a Judaism that is renewing itself. It seems to me that there is a question which is the same for all of Europe; are we able to develop a European perspective, a European Jewish perspective, in which among other things women are regarded as equal? Europe is important to me, because it is not possible simply to translate Israeli or American Judaism into our context. In Israel a specific form of secular Judaism has developed, and we cannot compare even the role of religious Judaism, Orthodoxy in particular, which is almost a state religion, with the situation in Europe. As far as the USA is concerned, religion shapes public life there in a way that is very different from here. There is a specific form of spirituality, which starts with 'faith in oneself' and leads to a general social religiousness, expressed in the 'American Dream'. This too we cannot simply translate into our European context. Authentic Judaism is important to me – of course we can import rabbis from abroad,

rabbis who bring with them a much more positive understanding of what it means to be Jewish than that of European Jews, but I think it is more appropriate that rabbis come from the respective contexts, are aware of their problems and learn to offer authentic responses to them.

Europe has become an issue for me not least through the formation of 'Beit Debora', a network of Jewish women rabbis, female cantors and scholars.[8] In Europe belonging to a country and to its national history is of great importance, particularly belonging to a linguistic community, for within languages lie cultures and their differences. In Europe we have a history of nations being at war against each other, we have a history of Jews being persecuted, a history of tensions within Judaism. This is where the details of our formation are different, we are something special – and the question is whether we will be able to develop a European Jewish perspective which refers to our context. The Netherlands are possibly a good place for this, because this country has always shown that it is particularly open to new developments.

What are the issues in which you in your current situation would like to be involved? What are your particular concerns at the moment?
Women in roles of leadership and the ethical justification of power – that is my topic.[9] The central issue is always the question of power: who in society is in a position of power, of power with regard to definitions, structures, forms? Women should have the confidence to exercise power, they ought to be in positions of power and this means to take on responsibility, having to make decisions, indeed 'to become guilty', not to be content with the role of the victim ('it is always someone else's fault'), but also not to become cynical ('we just have to live with being guilty'); it means to be bound ethically – this is important to me. We cannot do this, I think, without religion: there is a text, there are interpretations, an ethic – there is a point of reference, there is a corrective for one's own desire for power. And finally: there is a highest authority, God, before whom we all stand. Everything is not just within ourselves, rather it has to be measured by a general standard.

I want to conclude with a prayer that has been formative for me. It is by Bertha Bettelheim, the founder of the Jewish women's movement:

Call

My God, you are not a God of
gentleness, of the word and of incense,
not a god of the past.

You are a God who is present always and everywhere.
You are a God who demands from me;
Through your commandments I am made holy;
You expect me to choose between good and evil;
You demand me to show that I am strength of your strength,
to be minded towards you above me, to take others with me,
to help with all that I am.
Demand, demand,
so that with every breath of my life my conscience senses,
there is a God.

14 November 1935[10]

The interview was conducted by Marie-Theres Wacker who also edited this contribution.

Translated by Natalie K. Watson

Notes

1. A Jewish movement in the USA which understands Judaism not as a 'religion' but as a 'civilization'. Its founder was Mordecai Kaplan (1881–1983).
2. See www.aleph.org.
3. Elisa Klapheck (ed.), 1999, *Fräulein Rabbiner Jonas, 'Kann die Frau das rabbinische Amt bekleiden?'*, Teetz: Hentrich & Hentrich.
4. Judith Plaskow, 1991, *Standing Again at Sinai: Judaism from a Feminist Perspective*, San Francisco: Harper & Row; Susannah Heschel (ed.), 1983, *On Being a Jewish Feminist*, New York: Schocken Books; Pnina Nave Levinson, 1992, *Eva und Ihre Schwestern: Perspektiven einer jüdisch-feministischen Theologie*, Gütersloh: Gütersloher Verlagshaus.
5. Cf. for example Daniel Boyarin, 1993, *Carnal Israel: Reading Sex in Talmudic Culture*, Berkeley: University of California Press. It might be of particular interest for Christian readers that Boyarin also wrote an interpretation of Paul; cf. Daniel Boyarin, 1994, *A Radical Jew: Paul and the Politics of Identity*, Berkeley: University of California Press.
6. Except when a man converts. In Chassidic Judaism the tradition is that men go into the *mikwa* at the beginning of the Sabbath.
7. See www.hagalil.com/europa/holland.htm. There is, however (so far), no mention of Beit Ha'Chidush Amsterdam.
8. *Beit Debora* Issues 1 and 2 (2000 and 2001) can be ordered from L.Daemmig@t-online.de (please include a donation).
9. Cf. Elisa Klapheck, 2003, 'Ester und Amalek', in Katharina von Kellenbach et al. (eds), 2003, *Von Gott reden im Land der Täter: theologische Stimmen der dritten Generation seit der Shoah*, Darmstadt: Wissenschaftliche Buchgesellschaft.

10. Reprinted in Elisa Klapheck and Lara Dämmig (eds), 2003, *Bertha Pappenheim: Gebete / Prayers*, Teetz: Hentrich & Hentrich.

II. Christianity

Christianity and Feminism among the Babukusu of Western Kenya

ANNE NASIMIYU-WASIKE

Before I discuss feminism and Christianity among the Babukusu of Western Kenya, where I come from, I would like to define what I understand by feminism. In my understanding, feminism advocates equal opportunities for all women and men in all areas of life in order to foster human relationships characterized by freedom and mutuality.[1] It is a call to authentic Christian living and is pro-human.[2] Feminism aims at liberating the human community from entrenched attitudes and structures that cannot operate unless dichotomies and hierarchies are maintained. It is concerned with the whole of the human community in which female and male humanity shape a balanced community within which each and every person experiences fullness of being. It calls for the inclusion of women into the community of interpretation and women's experiences to become an integral part of the definition of being human.[3] Feminism is opposed to discrimination on the basis of gender. It opposes any ideology, belief, attitude or behaviour that establishes or reinforces such discrimination.

The Babukusu are a patriarchal society with legal, economic, political, religious and cultural systems in which members of the male sex have complete control over women. This is to the advantage of men and to the disadvantage of women.

I grew up in a family of six boys and four girls. The girls were born first and I was the second-born daughter. My parents were fervent and committed Catholics. They did not have formal western education themselves but they ensured that all their children had access to it. My father made sure that all the children went to good schools. The boys attended Catholic day schools and the girls were taken to convent boarding schools to ensure that we studied well and without distractions.

During holidays all of us children helped our parents on the farm. When the farm work was over, the girls had to assist our mama to fetch water, collect firewood and prepare food for the family. Meanwhile, the boys cleaned themselves and rested, waiting to be served by the female members of the family. Once I complained to my mother as to why my brother was not helping me to fetch firewood. My mother responded by telling me that my duty as a woman was to serve *basila mbele* ('people without breasts'). This raised some resentment within me but I still felt helpless in the given situation. From childhood girls are socialized to view themselves as dependent, as caregivers, and as subservient beings. It is the women themselves who teach this to their daughters. In my case it was my mother who insisted that I do what women are expected to do in our tradition. Many times I complained and rebelled against the expected norms.

My mother had a very difficult time and often worried about me and my future life. This was because a Babukusu woman's social purpose and maturity was grounded in her productive and reproductive powers. My aunt Kesia Nabalayo was the first highly educated woman in my mother's clan. She was a very independent person and when she completed her college education she was employed in a nearby school as a teacher. Everybody began to whisper as to why she was not married and yet she was mature. Men of about her age would come to visit her but none would qualify to enter into a relationship with her. She was seeking a relationship of mutual partnership but none of the men was ready for this kind of a relationship. One would hear the men comment that marrying this lady was like marrying another man. This was because she was not conforming to the traditional expectation of a woman in the society. Kesia Nabalayo rejected the traditional concept of a man paying bride wealth for the woman and the more educated a woman is the more expensive she becomes. The parents of Kesia wanted her to get married so that she would remove the *luswa* (curse) from the home and enrich the family with the bride wealth. Traditionally, every normal woman had to get married, for the woman's maturity and fulfilment was in marrying and bearing children. Instead Kesia chose to buy twelve cows for her parents and she purchased twenty-five acres of land away from home for her own settlement. Kesia did not consider herself a feminist, but her actions strongly supported feminist ideals. When I decided to become a nun at the age of fifteen, she was the only person in my whole extended family who supported me. She believed that as a nun I would not suffer under male domination. Little did she know that even in the Church the decisions are made by men.

I will now briefly look at some of the traditional African expectations of women and their roles in society and then trace some of the changes taking place in the present.

Family and religion in the African tradition

The African religious heritage laid great emphasis on family and religion. It was the extended family, the clan and the ethnic community which took care of the production and distribution of services and goods. Ethnic taboos and values maintained the community's law and order. Deviants were punished according to the gravity of the offence. The elders of the ethnic group trained the youth in the ways and wisdom of the society. Jobs were defined according to gender and age categories. It would be demeaning for one to attempt a job outside his/her age and sex categories.[4]

The religious system was more than a way of relating to God. It encompassed all other aspects of human life. Life was seen as a profoundly religious phenomenon and was lived in a religious universe. This notion was captured in the African myths, customs, traditions, beliefs, moral actions and social relationships. Every ethnic group in Africa has its own religious wisdom and tradition which is passed on from one generation to another in its prayers, wise sayings, idioms, myths, legends, stories, proverbs and oral history. When Christianity came to Africa, it found this rich fertile ground in which to plant itself. Unfortunately the evangelizers did not take into account this African religious heritage. Instead of planting Christianity in the African religious system by way of enculturation, they established a parallel religious system with its own male-dominated hierarchies.

Women as mothers

In traditional Africa a woman was always seen as mother of the family, the clan and the ethnic group. Among the Babukusu, the children were named according to the clan of the mother. For example, the great Babukusu prophet Elijah Masinde was always called Elijah wa Nameme. Nameme is the clan of the mother of Elijah Masinde. In the whole of Black Africa a woman is seen as a sacred vessel of life. Within herself she carries both male and female life. The female child carries for the community the hope of its continuity, for she will issue forth from herself life of both males and females into the world. She gives life, nourishment, warmth and protection to all. In the realm of fertility women's roles and images are noble. Unfortunately, outside influences and harsh economic realities have eroded this value.

Today poor families see the girl child mainly as a source of wealth for the family.

Traditionally, there were no children without fathers or mothers. Children were always a welcome blessing whether born in or out of wedlock and the uncles and aunts became the mothers and fathers of these children. Today the streets of most towns in Kenya are full of street children whom society no longer regards as a blessing but as a curse. These children without anyone to care for them come from various backgrounds. Some are orphans, others are children of single parents who are unable to cope with the harsh economic and social pressures and their children have to fend for themselves. Other children just run away from home due to bad social influences.

In addition, women and children were never killed even in war times because killing women and girl children was, in effect, killing humanity. Today this value has been so eroded that during ethnic clashes in Kenya, women and children, even babies, were slaughtered without any mercy. Nevertheless, the notion of motherhood is still highly exalted in African communities. A mother is held in the highest esteem and her role cannot be duplicated or replaced in one's life. A woman who is not married has no status in the African traditional world-view.

This is why Kesia Nabalayo could not be left in peace when she was of age and not married. Christianity introduced the celibate religious life which has been accepted and many women and men have embraced it. This gives status to the unmarried who consecrate their lives to God in the service of God's people. The people have come to accept this consecrated unmarried life and they pray that at least one of their children will be called to this way of life.

Women as religious leaders

In traditional societies women played important roles in religious activities. They were medicine women who acted as healers and counsellors. There were also women priests, diviners, seers, rainmakers and mediums. Although in most cases the women's ministrations were limited to other women and children, there were times when women mediums communicated divine messages to the whole community. In traditional Africa both women and men were equally recognized as worthy instruments through whom the divine communicates with humanity and people communicate with the divine. This recognition of women and men as worthy instruments of God was rejected by the Christian evangelizers of Africa. The churches opposed all forms of African women priests and prophets.[5] Women's ministerial roles in African religious tradition were much more of a characteristic nature than of a clerical one. This is a value in African religious tradition which could have enriched Christianity by giving it a balanced and equal recognition of both men and women as worthy members of society whom God can choose to use in religious functions.

Women as sources of wealth

The image of a woman as source of wealth for her community is found in most patriarchal societies in Africa. In some communities marriage was contracted at an early stage of the baby's life. In most cases the would-be husbands were much older than the girls because young men had to postpone marriage until they acquired enough wealth in the form of cattle, sheep, goats and other commodities to exchange them for a wife. Today young women and men are opting to cohabit. They refer to this way of living as 'come we stay' philosophy. This phenomenon is very common among the youth and living together can take as long as ten years before the marriage can be formalized. This is the time the young couple saves for the bride-wealth. Even the Church cannot allow young people to receive the sacrament of marriage until the traditional rituals and rites are completed.

The traditional bride-wealth concept, however, is giving way to new understandings. Some Christian-educated parents are instead supporting the new couple by assisting them economically to settle and others are just requesting a small token as a symbolic gift to represent the bride-wealth. But rural communities still adhere to the traditional understanding of bride-wealth and here the women are wholly subservient to their husbands. Educated and enlightened Christian women are seeking much more recognition as persons in their own right in relation to men and other persons in society. They are seeking equal, mutual partnership in marriage and in all other relationships. This is the reason why Kesia Nabalayo could not find a man who could meet her expectations in a relationship.

In my tradition, as in most patriarchal ethnic communities in Africa, polygamy is practised. Polygamy is based on the subservient relationship that already exists between a man and a woman. Even some Christians practise polygamy. It is up to women to reject this practice by refusing to be second or third wives.

Obstacles to women in my tradition

In my tradition there are several obstacles that hamper women from actual-izing their potential. First, due to a long period of male dominance, women have come to accept their subjugation as their destiny. It is the women who reject their fellow women who try to challenge the status quo. They have come to believe that traditions must be observed and maintained. They are the ones who sneak out their girl children at night to undergo female genital mutilation since the practice is discouraged by the government.

Second, the woman's role as mother is very much highlighted and mature girls are pressured by the society to get married. Young girls drop out of school to get married and some drop out due to pregnancy out of wedlock. This latter group is stigmatized by the community and often ends up in abject poverty.

Third, the woman's role as caregiver, especially during this time of HIV/AIDS, has disadvantaged the girl child. When the father of the family is sick, the mother of the family takes care of him, but when the mother of the family is sick, it is the girl child who takes care of the mother. Girl children are often forced out of school in order to provide care for their ailing parents, siblings or relatives.

Fourth, although there is general acceptance that women and men are equal before God, the Church and the society still favour men over women. Finally, educated young women frequently opt for single life in order to pursue their individual development and fulfilment. Such women experi-ence discrimination in some companies which choose only to employ married women.

Signs of hope

It is encouraging to see that more and more women are getting educated and some are raising questions that cannot be ignored by the Church and the society. These women see women's rights as human rights. Therefore, the Church and society have to defend all human rights. Human rights are about human dignity. The Church and the society have to create conditions that enable all persons to live in dignity by virtue of their being human and created in the image and likeness of God (Gen. 1.26).

Second, there are organizations which watch and monitor human rights violations in the country. These bodies are challenging political, economic and social functioning that discriminate and deny some people their basic rights to food, water, shelter, clothing, education, employment opportuni-

ties and access to affordable drugs, especially those suffering from HIV/
AIDS-related diseases. They also speak up against cases of forced child
labour, rape and violence against those who are vulnerable and marginalized
in the society. The Kenya National Commission on Human Rights
(KNCHR) affirms that eternal vigilance is what we need if each person's
dignity and rights are to be upheld.[6] This affirmation emphasizes the biblical call to all people that we should watch out for each other, by speaking out
and up and condemning acts that violate the basic rights of the vulnerable
and the weak in the society. These thorny issues must continue to be
addressed so that there is a high level of awareness in the society. The fact
that I think that there is hope for a more humane future society gives me a
sense of fulfilment.

In my tradition leadership in the society was a male prerogative. Women
could only be leaders of women and children. Women's religious leadership
roles enabled them to participate equally in traditional religious matters.
Christianity did not accept this kind of leadership by women. There have
been efforts to include women in decision-making positions in society. In
government women constitute about 10 per cent of the leadership. Hopefully with the making of the new constitution women will play key roles in all
decision-making situations, perhaps even in the Church.

Women like Kesia Nabalayo are continuing to act bravely in society,
hence demonstrating women's critical discernment as moral agents of
change. These women's radical defiance challenges those traditions that are
limiting and binding for women. I see such a heritage as a process of self-
empowerment. It informs us that these individual stories should not be lost
but recorded for the inspiration and benefit of the whole Church and society.

Some of the central questions for me in my context as I reflect on my dual
religious traditional heritage are based on the need to expand our Christian
identity in order to generate a much more inclusive Christian theology than
the one we have inherited.

In the first place, there is need to shift our attention from the Bible and the
Christian tradition to people's stories. This is because the Bible and the
Christian tradition often ignored women's experiences. We have to believe
that God's manifestations are not only found in the Bible and the early
Christian tradition but that God's revelation is also found in images and
metaphors used to talk about God in other religious traditions. It is important to tap our African religious traditional heritage so that our religious and
cultural heritage becomes a vehicle for knowing and appreciating God. Our
Christian identity has to expand by opening us to other rich manifestations
in other cultural contexts that reveal the divine in our world. Enculturation

is a dynamic process, which unfolds with the change of culture. The theology of enculturation has to become an ongoing critical process of theologizing through which Christian identity is contextualized within the cultural forms and social institutions of other cultural heritages. This is Christianity reaching people in their most profound experiences of life, and making possible the widespread contribution of all cultural values in the source of the gospel.

Second, the Church must prolong the incarnation of Christ in time and space. The Church's religious celebrations must be embedded in the culture and traditions of the people. As African women theologians we have to move from passive reception of traditional Christian theology to an active critical construction of our own theology based in our African integral holistic understanding of life. We have to learn the wisdom of our own people so that it can form the matrix of our theologizing. African Christian women have to find their own way of speaking about God. They have to create new models, new concepts and new symbols which express their own religious vision. African women's theology has to weave its traditional religious heritage and Christian heritage in new ways of naming their God, naming themselves and naming their world.

The third issue for African women theologians is to create a theological discourse that is centred in a plurality of voices and which displays the genuine universality of the Church. Such a discourse recognizes the creation of ethno-theologies which lie in the praxis of the religious communities struggling for the liberation of humanity. All theologies must contribute to the liberation and humanization of the human family and the articulation of human compassion for justice, peace and reconciliation of people and their environment.

Gender studies have been initiated in all public state universities in Kenya. This has helped in gender mainstreaming in education and in society. Although in the departments of religious studies, introductory courses on African Women's Theology have been established, there is still a need to establish departments of African Women's Theology in these institutions of higher learning, so that those wishing to specialize in African Women's Theology can do so.

I would like to end by sharing a poem written by Nancy R. Smith which captures the need for gender mainstreaming in every aspect of human life:

For every woman who is tired of acting weak when she knows she is strong, there is a man who is tired of appearing strong when he feels vulnerable.

For every woman who is tired of acting dumb,
there is a man who is burdened with the constant expectation of
'knowing everything.'

For every woman who is tired of being called 'an emotional female,'
there is a man who is denied the right to weep and to be gentle.

For every woman who is called unfeminine when she competes,
there is a man for whom competition is the only way to prove his
masculinity.

For every woman who is tired of being a sex object,
there is a man who must worry about his potency.

For every woman who feels 'tied down' by her children,
there is a man who is denied the full pleasures of shared parenthood.

For every woman who is denied meaningful employment or equal pay,
there is a man who must bear full financial responsibility for another
human being.

For every woman who was not taught the intricacies of an automobile,
there is a man who was not taught the satisfactions of cooking.

For every woman who takes a step toward her own liberation,
there is a man who finds the way to freedom has been made a little easier.[7]

Notes

1. Francine Cardman, 1980, 'Feminism and Faith' *Leadership Conference of Women Religious Newsletter* 8/2, p. 1.
2. Anne Nasimiyu-Wasike, 1988, *A Report on ANA's Second Polygamy Consultation*, Nairobi, Kenya, p.1.
3. Mercy Amba Oduyoye, 2000, *Hearing and Knowing: Theological Reflections on Christianity in Africa*, Nairobi: Acton Publishers, p. 121.
4. William C. Bier (ed.), 1968, *Woman in Modern Life*, New York: Fordham University Press, p. 56.
5. *Pro Mundi Vita Dossiers*: 'Contribution to the Rights and Wrongs of African Women' *African Dossier* 9, Brussels 1979, p. 8.
6. *IMARA*, Newsletter of the Association of Sisterhoods of Kenya, Justice and Peace Commission AOSK-JPC News Link 36 (July/Aug. 2005), p. 1.
7. http://www.workplacespirituality.info/ForEveryWoman.html Copyright © 1973 Nancy R. Smith.

Women and the Church:
A Greek Orthodox Perspective

KATERINA KARKALA–ZORBA

There is no longer Jew or Greek, there is no longer slave or free, there is no longer male and female; for all of you are one in Christ Jesus. (Gal. 3.28, NRSV)

There is probably no other text which has received so much attention from interpreters with regard to the equality of men and woman as this passage from the apostle Paul's epistle to the Galatians.[1] And no other text has probably been so badly misunderstood. The emphasis, as I see it, is less on the sameness of men and women, but on the unity of all in Jesus Christ. The original Greek text does not say 'men' and 'women' but 'male' and 'female'. This means: in Jesus Christ there is no discrimination on the basis of difference between the sexes but unity.

Here one could point to the creation of men and women (Gen. 1.26f.). What we find here is one human being created in the image of God. Men and women are called to be in the image of God who with the Holy Spirit is in communion with the Son of God, the Son of Man who has taken up within himself the whole of humanity.[2] According to Gregory of Nazianzus men and women were made by one and the same creator, all are made from the same dust, in the same image, will die the same death and be raised by the same resurrection. According to Gregory, the law that God has given is just, only human law-givers create injustice, for they are all male, hence 'the law is biased against women'.[3] The unity anticipated by Paul will resolve such inequalities, yet it will not dissolve the personal characteristics of each individual. Rather they should work together and with each other and complement each other.

Being a woman in the Orthodox Church

The Orthodox Church understands itself as a Church in which the Tradition, but also true teaching and the true expression of this teaching (*orthē doxa*), play a very important part. As in all Christian churches so also in the Orthodox Church women are bearers of the faith and have throughout history and over the centuries made their contribution to the building up of the faith.[4]

The Church does not lack images of women: we find women depicted on icons on the iconostasis in front of the altar as well as on frescos on the walls. There are sufficient role models: holy mothers and holy women from the early Church and the Church of the first millennium, the martyrs and great-martyrs, such as Katharina, Marina, ordinary women religious, abbesses and also other holy women who walked in the way before us. These saints are not merely images of fiction, but they come to life, as it were, in the action of the liturgy as well as in the lives of individuals, for example as patron saints. Holy women like holy men have their firm place in the liturgical calendar of the Orthodox Church. In addition, there are moveable women's feasts in the calendar of Easter, such as the Feast of the Myrrh-Bearing Women (on the second Sunday after Easter) or the Feast of the Samaritan Woman who had a theological conversation with Jesus at the well (on the fourth Sunday after Easter). Among all the saints (male and female), however, Mary, the Mother of God, the *Panhagia* (the All Holy One) has a special place. She is the prototype of the spiritual perfection of humanity,[5] she is the New Eve, in whom the biblical vision of God and creation as an act of love finds expression.[6] She is the deacon of our salvation,[7] who wants to bring us humans closer to Christ.

In the life of the Church women have an important place. They are the ones who establish and maintain the family's relationship to church life. When it comes to preparing for the sacraments such as baptism, marriage and funerals, they have particular, frequently traditional, roles. Also, on particular days of prayer more women can be seen in church, such as on the four Fridays during Great Lent before Easter, when the *Chairetismoi* (words of greeting) to Mary are sung and the service concludes with the *Akathistos* hymn. The same applies also during the fifteen days before the Feast Day of the Ascension of Mary when we sing the Great and the Small Prayer of Intercession to Mary (the so-called *Parakletiki*).

In the Orthodox Church it is still the case today that women are the ones who within the family or in private life dare go to church and also involve their families in it. For many people it was women, their mothers, grandmothers, godmothers, aunts, elder sisters and so on who introduced them to the faith. Women as those who initiate into the faith, be it within the family, in school, as well as generally in secular society, are likely to remain important in the future. However, in order to make this possible and to make it easier for younger women to participate in the life of the Church, the Church has to have the courage to take a number of important steps.

Positions of leadership in the Orthodox Church

In the Orthodox Church responsibilities with regard to the liturgy and the sacraments are not ordered according to power. The bishop as the president of the eucharistic *synaxis* is the 'first among equals'. The people of God, men and women, participate in the liturgy, which as the work (*ergon*) of the people (*laos*) is carried out by all the people. Therefore the different offices are seen as complementing each other and not as super- or sub-ordinate to each other.

The fact that more and more women study theology leads to women having the same opportunities available to them with regard to teaching in schools as their male colleagues. Here we have to take into account that for the Orthodox Church studying theology is not the same as training for the priesthood. For the latter there are seminaries where this training is possible for deacons and priests. Deacons and priests frequently complete their theological studies after they have been ordained. Men and women who have studied theology normally become teachers of religious education in secondary schools.

Here we must make particular reference to the 'Particular Concern' in the Final Report of the Inter-Orthodox Theological Consultation, which took place in Rhodes in 1988, and which among other things pleaded for a fuller participation of women in the life of the Church.[8] This also includes a more active participation of male and female lay theologians in church institutions and decision-making bodies. The Synod of the Church in Greece works with commissions which include theologians, scholars and experts on particular issues. These commissions advise the Synod in making important decisions such as, for example, questions of bioethics, of ecumenical relationships, and even with regard to women's issues.

The fact that most parish priests are married highlights the role of the priest's wife or *presbytera* in the life of the parish. Without her consent no married candidate for the priesthood can be admitted to the priestly office. In the parish, her role is regarded as complementing the role of the priest. In many parts of Greece people not only kiss the hand of the priest but also that of his wife. She is a point of contact for many parishioners if the priest is not around, or some even prefer to contact his wife first. However, the role of the priest's wife has changed in recent years. Among the reasons for this are changes in patterns of living – frequently the priest no longer lives within his parish – and also the fact that the majority of priests' wives want to follow their own career. On the whole it has become more difficult for candidates for the priesthood to find a wife who agrees to become the wife of a priest. Consequently many men who want to become priests are unmarried when they are ordained (and, according to the Orthodox tradition, have to remain so). The Orthodox Church will have to think about exploring ways of making the role of the priest's wife more attractive. At the same time new ways will have to be found to create opportunities for theologically educated women to develop their abilities and gifts in areas such as theology, pastoral theology, social work and education. This will certainly be a task for the years to come.

The office of deaconesses and the question of women's ordination

The Orthodox Church does recognize the ordination of women, to the office of deaconess. This is an office which was known in the early Church and in the Byzantine Empire. According to Evangelos Theodorou, whose 1954 dissertation was about 'The "ordination" or the "laying on of hands" of deaconesses',[9] 'deaconesses . . . were without a doubt regarded as clergy in the Eastern Churches and were the only "táxis" or stage of the ordained female ecclesial office that belonged to the diaconate in its own right'.[10] Thus the ordination of deaconesses is absolutely equal to the ordinations of higher clerics, i.e., deacons, presbyters and bishops. The office of the female deacon is to be regarded as equal to the male diaconate, for it is an 'ordination' and not a 'laying on of hands'.[11]

During the twentieth century there were several attempts at reviving the office of deaconess. In Russia at the beginning of the twentieth century there were several supporters of the office of deaconess, such as Bishop Stefan of Mogilev, Mother Ekaterina of Lesna, Archpriest Aleksii Maltsev, the Russian priest of Berlin and Bishop Evlogy, who later become the Exarch of the Ecumenical Patriarchate for the Russian Orthodox Churches in Western Europe. The efforts of the Grand Princess Elisabeth Fedorovna and later Mother Maria Skobtsova, only recently canonized as a saint, point to the fact that they held an office similar to that of a deaconess.[12]

On Pentecost Sunday 1911 on the Greek island of Aegina Bishop

Nektarios consecrated a nun to be a deaconess. Although the hierarchy of the day was critical of this, Bishop Nektarios is now recognized as a saint and is much loved in Greece and in other Orthodox Churches. In addition, Evangelos Theodorou proves that there were several convents in Greece where women religious were consecrated to be deaconesses.[13]

The liturgical responsibilities of deaconesses were to be seen as combining charity/*diakonia* and liturgy. Among the roles of deaconesses were the baptizing of women, the taking and distribution of communion to women who were sick and were unable to come to church, as well as ministries of love, service, mission, catechesis and teaching.

Thus the reintroduction of the office of deaconess is not a new issue for the Orthodox Church. More recently it was Theodorou who brought the question back on the agenda. The Inter-Orthodox Consultation, organized by the Ecumenical Patriarchate in Rhodes, proposed to revive the office and to adapt it to the new cultural situation.[14] The Greek American Orthodox theologian and psychologist Kyriaki Karidoyanes FitzGerald published a study on the subject with the title *Women Deacons in the Orthodox Church: Called to Holiness and Ministry*[15] and also translated some of the rites of consecration.[16]

In October 2004 the Synod of the Church in Greece discussed the 'role of women in the institution of the Church and the revival of the office of deaconesses'. In his introductory paper Metropolitan Chrysostomos of Chalkida said that 'a first step towards the revival of the office of deaconesses could be the ordination of selected nuns'.[17] However, it is still undecided if 'only those who are unmarried or widowed can be consecrated as deaconesses'[18] which could lead to a situation of inequality as male deacons may be married.

Also open is the much wider question about the ordination of women. On the one hand, the ordination to the office of deaconess is a *cheirotonia* (ordination) and not a mere laying on of hands (*cheirothesia*). This renders it 'entirely equal to the *cheirotoniai* of the higher ranks of the clergy (deacons, presbyters and bishops)'.[19] On the other hand the tradition of the Orthodox Church does not know of the ordination of women to the office of a priest or bishop.[20]

To this we can say: the Orthodox Church knows no limits to the expressions of the true faith and witness. This also applies to the question of the ordination of women.[21] The French Orthodox theologian Elisabeth Behr-Sigel has engaged deeply with the position of women in the Church. In her book *The Ministry of Women in the Church*[22] she argues openly for the ordination of women in the Orthodox Church. In the book which she co-authored together with Bishop Kallistos Ware[23] she wrote that the question about the ordination of women is no longer one which is merely raised 'from outside' of Orthodoxy, that is, from the wider ecumenical movement, but one that has also become an internal issue for the Orthodox Church.

Elisabeth Behr-Sigel died on 26 November 2005 at the age of 98 years. Until the end of her life she regarded the ordination of women as a hot topic of discussion for the ecumenical dialogue.[24] She was never satisfied with the simple argument that 'the Orthodox Church knows of no ordination of women to the priesthood',[25] but faced up to the challenges of modern times.

Feminist theology and the challenges to the Orthodox Church

We can assume that within Orthodox theology there is no systematic starting point for a feminist theology. Furthermore, Orthodox theologians even reject feminist theology as being 'western'. We would, however, need to ask if Orthodox theology could not at least offer to start a conversation with feminist theology in which we could not at least find elements of what it too is seeking to achieve. Here we could concede from an Orthodox point of view that the feminist critique of the patriarchal structures of the Orthodox Church[26] is accurate at least as far as its external structures are concerned. However, feminist theology could also form a channel of communication for a current theological approximation:[27]

- Instead of speaking, as our ecclesial tradition does, of God as a strict and vindictive judge, we could speak of the God of philanthropy, who loves human beings and comes to sinners.
- Instead of referring to God as ruler, we could talk about a God who wants to work together with human beings.
- Instead of a spirit–matter dualism, we could speak of healing matter in its entirety, of nature, of human beings, without condemning them as evil.
- Instead of a God who is transcendent, beyond the world and beyond humanity, we could speak of a God who acts in the world with his energies. It is the communion/*koinonia* of the three persons of the 'uncreated Trinity' which also serves as the image for the human communion of men and women, the 'created epiphany'[28] in our society.

According to the Catholic theologian Anne Jensen,[29] Greek Orthodox theology has preserved fundamental theological insights which could relate to the demands of women and move on the much more andro-centric western theological way of thinking in a way that is more healing. Once again I want to refer to the saints of the Christian Easter, for example the Mothers of the Church[30] alongside the Church Fathers, whose Lives and written works, where available, have increasingly been published in recent years.[31] This shows that not only men have shaped our faith but also women. These women frequently lived in the shadow of the Church Fathers, but in reality they had their part in the formation of the Christian community.

During about the last forty years the Orthodox Church has wanted to give its own answer to the current challenges, and in order to do so, it has initiated several consultations. Frequently these initiatives are to be seen as contributions of the Orthodox Church to the ecumenical dialogue and therefore took place in direct cooperation with the World Council of Churches. Among these are the women's consultation in the Romanian convent of Agapia in 1976 on 'Orthodox Women: their Role and Participation in the Orthodox Church', the 1990 'Inter-Orthodox Theological Consultation' in Rhodes, which has already been mentioned, and the Second International Orthodox Women's Consultation in 1990 at the Orthodox Academy of Crete on the theme of 'Church and Civilization'.[32] Two conferences of Orthodox and Old Catholic male and female theologians on 'The Role of Woman in the Church and the Ordination of Women as an Ecumenical Problem' took place in Livadia in Greece and in Poland;[33] two conferences in Damascus (1996) and in Istanbul (1997) discussed the topic 'Recognizing the Signs of the Times'[34]. We should also mention the journal *MaryMartha* which was published from 1991 to 1998 by the Australian Orthodox theologian Leonie Liveris. These consultations and initiatives have certainly resulted in the question of women being taken up anew. Thus also a dialogue was begun in order to interpret the role of women in the Orthodox Church with regard to today's reality.

Epilogue

In our postmodern times the Christian faith is in a crisis in which, in my view, Orthodoxy can and must 'recognize the signs of the times' and bear witness to the genuine equality of men and women.

Perhaps one of the signs can be a conference which will take place from 28–30 July 2006 in Aylesford, Kent (England). The topic will be 'Women and Men in the Church, What is our vocation and ministry within the Church, whether we are clergy or lay people, whether we are monastics, married or single?' The conference will be organized by the Orthodox Community of Saint John the Baptist whose leader Bishop Kallistos Ware is supposed to be very open to the ordination of women. Certainly the

Tradition as well as the experience of the theology of the Orthodox Church will play an important part in this. Perhaps the icon of the resurrection in the convent church St Saviour, Chora in Istanbul will help us to do this. It shows Christ drawing to himself both man and woman, for in him there is neither male nor female, for all are 'one in Jesus Christ' (Gal. 3.28).

Translated by Natalie K. Watson.

Notes

1. Cf. Evanthia Ch. Adamtziloglou, 1998, 'Οὐκ ἔνι ἄρσεν καί θῆλυ . . .', *Τα Βασιλικά Χαρίσματα των δύο φύλων* (*'No longer male and female': the Royal Talents of both Sexes*, Gal. 3.28c, Gen. 1.26–27), Thessaloniki: University Studio Press.
2. Elisabeth Behr-Sigel, 1987, *Le Ministère de la Femme dans l'Eglise*, Paris: Cerf, p. 48 (ET: 1991, *The Ministry of Women in the Church*, Wheathampstead: A. Clarke).
3. Gregory of Nazianzus, Speech 37.6 (*PG* 36) 289 BC.
4. Dimitrios Tsamis, 1990, *Mēterikon*, Thessaloniki, vols 1–6.
5. Eftichia Gioultsi, 2001, *Παναγία, Πρότυπο Πνευματικῆς Τελειόσεως* (*The Panhagia: Model of Spiritual Perfection*), Thessaloniki: P. Pournara.
6. Alexander Schmemann, 1995, *The Virgin Mary: Celebration of Faith, Sermons* Vol. 3, Crestwood, NY: St Vladimir's Seminary Press.
7. Katerina Karkala-Zorba, 'The Role of Women in the Orthodox Church Today', *MaryMartha* 5/1 (1996–7).
8. Cf. 'Die Stellung der Frau in der Orthodoxen Kirche und die Frage der Ordination von Frauen', Abschlussbericht einer Interorthodoxen Theologischen Konsultation, *UNA SANCTA*, 1989/3.
9. Evangelos Theodorou, 1954, *Ἡ "Χειροτονία" Ἡ "Χειροθεσία" τῶν Διακονισῶν* (*The "Ordination" or the "Laying on of Hands" of Deaconesses*), Athens; and, 1949, *Ἡρωΐδες τῆς Χριστιανικῆς Ἀγάπης* (*Heroines of Christian Love*), Athens.
10. Evangelos Theodorou, 1986, 'Das Priesteramt nach dem Zeugnis der Byzantinischen Liturgischen Texte', paper presented at the 'Ecumenical Symposium', Ratisbonne, July 1985, *ΘΕΟΛΟΓΙΑ* 57/1, p. 161.
11. Theodorou, 'Das Priesteramt', p. 160. See also 'Didascalia and Apostolic Constitutions', in Johannes Quasten (ed.), 1953, *Patrology*, vol. 2, Utrecht, pp. 137–52.
12. Hélène Arjakovsky-Klépinine, 2001, *Mère Marie Skobtsova – Le sacrement du frère*, Paris: Le sel de terre; Elisabeth Behr-Sigel, 1996, 'The Life of Maria Skobtsova – an Orthodox Nun', *MaryMartha* 4/2, p. 18; Sergei Hackel, 1981, *Pearl of Great Price: The Life of Mother Maria Skobtsova 1891-1945*, London: Darton, Longman & Todd; and, 1967, 'Mother Maria Skobtsova: Deaconess

Manquée?', *Eastern Churches Review* 1/13; Mother Maria Skobtsova, 2003, *Essential Writings*, Maryknoll: Orbis Books.

13. Theodorou, 1954, Ή "Χειροτονία", p. 95f.
14. Cf. Conclusions of the Consultation Report, VIII: The Diaconate and "Minor Orders" in Gennadios Limouris (ed.), 1992, *The Place of the Woman in the Orthodox Church and the Question of the Ordination of Women, Interorthodox Symposium, Rhodos, Greece, 30 October – 7 November 1988*, Katerini Tertios, p. 31.
15. Kyriaki Karidoyanes FitzGerald, 1999, *Women Deacons in the Orthodox Church, Called to Holiness and Ministry*, Brookline, MA: Holy Cross Orthodox Press.
16. Karidoyanes FitzGerald, 1999, *Women Deacons*, pp. 59, 78.
17. Paper presented on 8 October 2004 at the Holy Synod of the Church of Greece: 'The Role of Women in the Whole Institution of the Church, Revival of the Institution of Deaconesses'.
18. 'The Role of Women'.
19. Theodorou, 1986, 'Das Priesteramt', p. 160.
20. Evangelos Theodorou, 2004, 'Oi diakonisses stēn istoria tēs Ekklēsias' ('The Deaconesses in the History of the Church'), in Metropolis von Dimitrias (ed.), 2004, Φύλο καί Θρησκεία, ἡ θέση τῆς Γυναίκας στήν ἐκκλησία (*Gender and Religion: The Role of Women in the Church*), Athens: Indiktos.
21. Thomas Hopko, 1999, *Women and Ordination*, New York: St Vladimir's Seminary Press.
22. See note 2.
23. Elisabeth Behr-Sigel, 1998, *L'ordination de femmes dans l' Église Orthodoxe*, Paris: Cerf.
24. Elisabeth Behr-Sigel, 2001, 'L'ordination des femmes: Un point chaud du dialogue oecuménique', *Contacts* 195.
25. See Epiphanius of Salamis, quoted in 'L'ordination des femmes'.
26. Anne Jensen, 1985, 'Wie patriarchalisch ist die Ostkirche? Frauenfragen in der orthodoxen Theologie', *UNA SANCTA* 40, pp. 130–45.
27. Evanthia Adamtziloglou, 1997, 'Pheministikē Theologia, Rhēxē ē gephyra me tēn Ellēnorthodoxē Paradosē?' ('Feminist Theology: Break with or Bridge to Greek Orthodoxy?'), in, 1997, Ήσαν δέ ἐκεῖ γυναίκες πολλαί... (*Many Women Were There . . .*), Thessaloniki: Simbo, p. 151.
28. Thomas Hopko, 1983, 'On the Male Character of Christian Priesthood', in Thomas Hopko (ed.), 1983, *Women and the Priesthood*, Crestwood, New York: St Vladimir's Seminary Press, p. 100. In the new edition of the book (1999) there is also a new version of Thomas Hopko's essay 'Presbyter/Bishop: A Masculine Ministry', pp. 139ff.
29. Anne Jensen, 1996, *God's Self-Confident Daughters: Early Christianity and the Liberation of Women*, trans. O. C. Dean, Kampen: Kok Pharos and Louisville: Westminster John Knox.
30. Tsamis, 1990, *Mēterikon*.

31. Adamitziloglou, 1997, Ἦσαν δέ ἐκεῖ γυναῖκες πολλαί...

32. 'Orthodox Women's Consultation, Orthodox Academy of Crete, January 1990: Church and Culture, Ministry, Human Sexuality, Participation and Decision Making Archives', *MaryMartha* 1/1–3, 1991–92.

33. Agathaggelos Charamantidis (ed.), 2001, 'Ἡ Ὀρθόδοξη Γυναίκα στήν Ἐνωμένη Εὐρώπη', Πρακτικά Διορθοδόξου Εὐρωπαϊκοῦ Συνεδρίου (*Orthodox Women in a United Europe*), Report on an Inter-Orthodox European Conference, Katerini: Epektasis.

34. Kyriaki Karidoyanes FitzGerald (ed.), 1999, *Orthodox Women Speak*, Geneva: WCC Publications and Brookline MA: Holy Cross Orthodox Press.

Christian Churches at the Crossroads: Theological Reflections from Argentina, Latin America and the Caribbean

VIRGINIA R. AZCUY

Women's voices within the global movement for Third-World liberation have helped to stir up 'an irruption within the irruption' in the conscience of Christian churches.[1] The first recipients of pastoral preference were the poor, but we then saw the 'procession of oppression' – socio-economic, ethnic-racial, gender and others – in Rosemary Radford Ruether's phrase. This evolution, which came about interwoven with other theoretical and practical developments of a different order, shows that the Christianity of recent decades has proved capable of affective solidarity and effective commitment in the face of historical challenges related to human dignity. Nevertheless, this seems insufficient, taking into account the brutality of growing social exclusion and the pervasive inequality of all sorts. It may be that a more decisive religious and social vitality in the future will be linked, to a greater extent than people think, to a deep transformation in the churches and to a wisdom that knows how to integrate old and new, spiritual and social, divine and human, masculine and feminine. Only a just and full human life can be worthy of faith – at least from the viewpoint of a feminism that calls itself Christian.

Brief contextual indications

In the Latin American theological context, including Argentina to some extent, the wave of feminism has intermingled especially with those other waves of liberation and human rights since the mid-1980s and, more recently and to a lesser extent, with ecological movements. We might say that, over and above the variants of different positions,[2] a *movement of feminist liberation or a feminist movement of liberation* has been developing,[3] which had and has its points of contact with outlooks current in other contexts. In defining this movement, the use of 'feminist' implies a critical

analysis of the way 'women' and 'femininity' are spoken of in liberation theology, insofar as these concepts are often expressed in terms of a patriarchal
outlook. Reception of this movement within the Christian church sphere
has proved diverse: on the one hand, the context of poverty and exclusion
experienced in Latin America and the Caribbean calls for determined commitment and actions on behalf of justice and human advancement, which
means there is a continued need for a project of integral and overall liberation – beyond the specific courses included in the present agenda. On the
other hand, the current situation in our countries, in both the secular and the
religious spheres, means that liberation movements are going through a
critical phase, or at least a difficult and complex one, either on account of the
resistance they themselves provoke or through the structural challenges they
have to face. In this general framework, the progress and consolidation of
feminism show the same signs of *actuality and difficulty* as the movements
that develop under the aegis of liberation and human dignity; at the same
time, though, the pace of change is slower and the restrictions greater,
taking into account the androcentric direction of our cultures and, to a large
extent, of our religious traditions. In Argentina, the relatively late arrival of
women in a theological tradition not yet four decades old[4] means that the
dominant discourses and practices still do not allow for a relatively full and
equitable participation by women: the primacy of a mostly implicit *theology
of women*,[5] the influence of *Marian devotions* adopted from theologies and
pastoral models that have not revised their anthropological approaches,[6] and
the recent emergence of *women with doctorates in theology* who can still not
find formal institutional positions of belonging and influence, are the basic
correlates from which the way unfolds.

As I see it, one the greatest difficulties in the Catholic sphere lies in the
clerical tendency of our churches, which continue to exalt ordained
Christian members over and above the baptized who carry out their vocation
in the form of a lay or consecrated life. That talk of *the situation of women in
the churches* should be an imperative for most of us women, while often
appearing to be a 'forced' subject for many of the men, shows that there is
still no deep understanding of this aspect of our reality. Our hopes grow, it
is true to say, when it is possible to make specific challenge visible in terms
of inequity, deficit or absence, when we can help to 'awaken' women so that
they can be generators of a new scenario more worthy of themselves, their
families and their faith communities. Our hope is also boosted through
meeting sisters and brothers who become 'fellow travellers' through their
search for fresh forms of relationship, mutual collaboration and exchange of
goods.

Basic aspirations: empowerment, sharing, leadership

Within the general concerns of a Catholic Church that is in the process of renewal, but which 'runs the risk of still showing a face with strongly hierarchical, clerical, and masculine features',[7] the theme of ministries is undoubtedly central to discussion and discernment. On the one hand, there is the question of a real and permanent recognition of *lay or baptismal ministries*, which is generally done partially and hesitantly; on the other, the more delicate and more widespread situation of *collaboration in the ordained pastoral ministry* or 'supply' ministries, which involves lay people – often married couples – and consecrated women. The situation of how far lay people can be ministers, and within this the question of women's ministries, seems directly to challenge the understanding and implementation of the communion dimension of the People of God.[8] In the Reformed churches, the number of women consecrated as pastors is growing, but this fact does not always mean their acceptance and positive evaluation by communities and their pastors.[9] In the field of theology, the overall situation of women is certainly one of 'underdevelopment'; that is, it is below a worthy level of minimum development, and this seems to call for specific decisions from institutional churches and their hierarchies.

This state of affairs does not, of course, mean that there is a complete absence of qualified and distinguished women theologians, but rather that their numbers are extremely limited. In the Final Document of the Second Latin American Meeting of Women Theologians of 1993, 'Entre la indignación y la esperanza' ('Between Indignation and Hope'), twelve women were mentioned as having achieved the grade of Doctor of Theology.[10] These figures reflect the fact that in some countries, such as Mexico, Peru and Paraguay, there is at present no formal academic sphere in which women can work according to their theological qualifications. Furthermore, there are few Latin American countries that have a woman citizen with a doctorate in theology residing in the country and active in the university sphere: the first two Mexican women with doctorates, Elsa Tamez (Methodist) and María Pilar Aquino (Roman Catholic), have emigrated, one to Costa Rica and the other to San Diego in the United States; the Cuban theologian Ada-María Isasi Díaz (Roman Catholic) has left her native country and currently lives in Drew in the USA; María Teresa Porcile (Roman Catholic), from Uruguay, died in 2001, leaving a major gap in the River Plate region. In some cases, the only woman with a doctorate comes from outside,[11] while in others we are witnessing the novelty of 'first conferral'.[12] In Brazil there are some notable early pioneers, such as María Clara Bingemer, Ana María

Tepedino and Ivone Gebara, together with numerous women theologians from the younger generation. At the Xaverian Catholic University of Bogotá the 'Theology and Gender' Research Group flourishes under the leadership of María del Socorro Vivas, Olga Vélez Caro and other women theologians. The past decade in Argentina has seen the formation of three mature women theologians' collectives active in various spheres: in university circles the 'Theology and Gender Forum' at ISEDET and the '*Teologanda*' Programme stand out;[13] in the field of education, catechesis and popular Bible reading there is the 'Rajab Theological Community' with its Biblical Team.[14] Finally, it is worth indicating the institutional leadership exercised by some women theologians in Latin America and the Caribbean as rectors or deans,[15] together with the growing number of women who have received their doctorate or are preparing for it. Nevertheless, despite all such efforts, we are very far from having brought about an academic and institutional development sufficient to speak of a significant presence of women theologians in universities, congregations, local churches and centres of pastoral formation and action. On the other hand, the Second Latin American and Caribbean Meeting, on the subject of 'Gender and Epistemology: Women and Disciplines', held in 1998, showed that confessional and non-confessional initiatives relating to women had registered an unprecedented advance: over twenty university courses on Gender and Women's Studies, in Mexico, Cuba, Nicaragua, Costa Rica, Panama, El Salvador, Guatemala, Ecuador, Peru, Bolivia, Brazil, Uruguay, Paraguay and Argentina, bore testimony to this spread.[16] This academic and institutional embedding of subjects related to women's lives and such gender representations undoubtedly favour acceptance and examination of these matters in the religious and theological spheres, at the same time encouraging greater interdisciplinary discussion.

Women's theologies in Argentina

In Argentina, and I think also in most Latin American and Caribbean countries, the main concern is to develop a real advancement of women so that they can be trained for and share in positions of intellectual, spiritual and pastoral leadership in communities and training establishments, particularly at tertiary and university level. In this respect, there are already certain initiatives in Buenos Aires aimed at responding to this need, in which the Evangelical Churches are taking part: the 'Theology and Gender Forum' is an activity of the extramural department of ISEDET; it seeks to reflect on and help other areas of academic and church life to establish more egalitarian political practices and world-views in gender terms. One part of this forum is its 'Permanent Seminary on Feminist Theory'.[17] Its being a 'forum' implies that it is a many-sided and multi-voiced meeting place, providing space for various groups and activities, among them a reflection and research seminar dedicated to studying feminist theory and outlook so as to approach them from the experience and discipline of each participant. In Nancy Bedford's view, philosophical feminism constitutes a real spur to theology: 'Speaking of "theological feminism" allows us to refer to a *movement* whose waves break constantly on the shore of theology, shaping it and changing it, whereas if we speak *only* of "feminist theology" it can look like a finished and wrapped product.'[18]

Besides this, in 2002 a group of mainly Catholic and some Evangelical women theologians began the *'Teologanda'* Programme of Studies, Researches, and Publications, which works through intensive open seminars, using visiting consultants from other disciplines together with a permanent group of researchers, with oversight from the theology faculties of the Argentine Catholic University of Buenos Aires, the University of El Salvador (San Miguel area) and other theological institutes of the region.[19] The programme seeks to contribute to the broad flow of 'theologies done by women', without canonizing any one position and allowing space for plurality and conversation; our consultants, together with a group of professionals from other disciplines, include a group of consultant (male) theologians from local institutions, which expresses the communal spirit of the collective. The subject chosen for study in the period 2003–05 was 'The journey of women in the theology of Latin America, the Caribbean, and the United States. Critical assessment and new perspectives';[20] in future, we want to broaden our studies geographically, paying special attention to other developing regions and to Europe. In the first three years of reflection, the *'teologandas'* have backed up their reading of women authors with inquiry into biographic and ethnographic methods, gender perspective, and feminism, which has given them a greater breadth and more depth in their theological approach. A basic question we women theologians of the 'intermediate' generation ask ourselves is how to succeed in consolidating our institutional appointments while at the same time keeping the autonomy we need: to do so, as in other contexts, we aim to keep up the spheres of forum, network and programme, which provide us with 'intermediate spaces' for growth and encounter. In the interior of the country, the faculty of philosophy at the Catholic University of Córdoba has, each year since 2003, held an interdisciplinary seminar on women.[21] There are growing prospects for interchange among the institutions mentioned; we are particularly interested in combining organizational efforts and offering career opportunities to postgraduate students.[22] The aim is always to open disciplinary and cross-disciplinary fields to promote discernment and transformation of human and social life in the direction of fuller, more just and more participatory forms; then to encourage, from the Christian churches, those spaces that generate thought and actions and can become part of a global programme of compassion and responsibility[23] that can be a major crossroads in hope for the future.

Translated by Paul Burns.

Notes

1. M. A. Oduyoye, 1994, 'Reflections from a Third World Woman's Perspective: Women's Experience and Liberation Theologies', in Ursula King (ed.), 1994, *Feminist Theology from the Third World: A Reader*, Maryknoll: Orbis; London: SPCK, pp. 23–34, here p. 24.
2. Theology from the woman's viewpoint, feminist theology of liberation, feminist theology in the various currents of eco-feminism, *mujerista*, Latina or Hispanic, womanist, or Afro-American. Personally, I have not included myself among 'women liberation theologians' or under the umbrella of 'feminist theology', but I have asked myself questions about women's lives, and I have tried to do theology from that hermeneutical background, in dialogue with feminism and with the tools necessary to discern, think and act more in conformity with the gospel.
3. Cf. Elina Vuola, 2002, *Limits of Liberation: Feminist Theology and the Ethics of Poverty and Reproduction*, Sheffield: Sheffield Academic Press.
4. The Argentine Theology Society has been meeting since 1971, and a group of women theologians spoke for the first time during the Twentieth Theology Week in 2001: see 'Panel: Iglesia, teología y mujeres', in Sociedad Argentina de Teología (ed.), 2002, *De la esperanza a la solidaridad*, Buenos Aires, pp. 195–250.
5. I refer to a patriarchal view of women, which assigns them their 'proper' roles, functions and spheres, subtly placing them in a position of inferiority or subordination compared to men.
6. Cf. V. R. Azcuy, 2004, 'Reencontrar a María come modelo. La interpretación feminista a la mariología actual', *Ephemerides Mariologicae* 54, pp. 69–72.
7. P. Coda, 2005, 'Cruzar el umbral de la reciprocidad', *Criterio* 2308, pp. 491–3, here p. 491.
8. Cf. Virginia R. Azcuy, 2005, 'Hacia una nueva imaginación sobre el laicado y las mujeres en la Iglesia', *Teología* 88, pp. 537–56. To see the ordination of women to the ordained ministry in the Catholic Church as the main question would be

to oversimplify the question; it is a matter of all the forms of mutuality and cooperation that are needed for communion in the pastoral sphere, of decision-making and reflection.

9. Cf. Nancy Bedford, 2000, 'La espiritualidad cristiana desde una perspective de género', *Cuadernos de Teología* 19, pp. 105–25, here p. 120ff.

10. Cf. A. M. Tepedino and M. P. Aquino (eds), 1998, *Entre la indignación y la esperanza: Teología Feminista Latinoamericana*, Bogotá, p. 198.

11. E.g., Anneliese Meis (German Catholic religious), professor at the Catholic University of Chile; in the same country, outside the academic sphere, there is the eco-feminist collective 'Con-spirando', including M. Judith Ress (US, lay Catholic), Ute Eibert-Cuadra (German Lutheran pastor) and Lene Sjørup (Danish Lutheran pastor); Antonieta Potente (Spanish Catholic) lectures at the Catholic University of Bolivia, and Barbara Andrade (German Catholic) at the Ibero-American University of Mexico. These names, and those listed below, are selective and not a complete list.

12. Iris Barrientos (Evangelical pastor), with a doctorate in biblical studies from ISEDET (Buenos Aires), is the first and only woman with this qualification in Honduras; María Angélica Otazú (lay Catholic) is the first Paraguayan woman with a doctorate, from Germany; Raquel Riquelme (Methodist pastor) comes from Chile and has a doctorate from Brazil.

13. Respective women at these bodies with doctorates are: Nancy Bedford (lay Baptist) living in Chicago but invited lecturer at ISEDET (www.isedet.edu.ar); Mercedes García Bachmann (Lutheran pastor), biblicist, professor at and dean of ISEDET; and Virginia R. Azcuy (Catholic consecrated), general coordinator of '*Teologanda*' (www.teologanda.com.ar). Heike Walz (Lutheran pastor) and Clara M. Temporelli (Catholic religious) have recently joined.

14. Its members are on leave from theological faculties and institutes and are pastorally involved in local church communities and collaborate in the mission of various religious Congregations, and share experiences in popular education and ecumenism (www.rajab.com.ar).

15. Elsa Tamez, Rector of the Latin American Biblical University in Costa Rica, member of the Ecumenical Research Department (DEI), theological assessor to Latin American Council of Churches (CLAI), besides contributing to journals and networks; María Clara Bingemer, Dean of the Pontifical Catholic University of Rio de Janeiro and organizer of the Loyola Centre for Faith and Culture; María García Bachmann, Dean of the Evangelical University Institute (ISEDET) of Buenos Aires, organizer, with María Strizzi, of the 'Theology and Gender' Forum, and member of the editorial board of *Cuadernos de Teología*; Iris Barrientos, Rector of the Theological Seminary of Honduras and national organizer of the Pastoral Agents' Network, among other posts.

16. Cf. S. Montesinos and A. Obach (eds), 1999, *Género y epistemología: Mujeres y disciplinas*, Santiago. The meeting was organized by the Interdisciplinary Programme for Gender Studies (PIEG).

17. N. Bedford, M. García Bachmann and M. Strizzi (eds), 2005, *Puntos de Encuentro*, Buenos Aires, p. 7.

18. N. Bedford, 'Presentación: Puntos de apoyo de los *Puntos de encuentro*', in *Puntosde encuentro*, p. 32.

19. Works already published by this collective are: V. R. Azcuy (ed.), 2001, 'El lugar teológico de las mujeres. Un punto de partida', *Proyecto* 39; V. R. Azcuy (ed.), 2004, 'En la encrucijada del género: Conversaciones entre teología y disciplinas', *Proyecto* 45.

20. The collective researches carried out are being published in four volumes: a bibliographic dictionary of women authors; an anthology of texts, with commentary; a list of studies on women writers; a volume of assessment and outlook. The managing editor of the project is V. R. Azcuy.

21. The first three were carried out and their proceedings edited by the dean of the university: C. Schickendantz (ed.), 2003, *Mujeres, género y sexualidad: Una Mirada interdisciplinary*, Córdoba; 2004, *Religión, género y sexualidad: Análisis interdisciplinares*, Córdoba; and 2005, *Cultura, género y homosexualidad: Estudios interdisciplinares*, Córdoba.

22. To sustain these initiatives financially, we seek to join personal and institutional resources; in the case of '*Teologanda*', I must acknowledge the academic and financial support through scholarships supplied by German–Latin American Cultural Exchange (ICALA), the Forum of German Catholic Women Theologians (AGENDA), the Wolfsburg Academy, and ADVENIAT. At the same time, we are trying to become self-sufficient financially through broadcasts, workshops and conferences.

23. See J. B. Metz, L. Kudd and A. Weisbrod (eds), 2000, *Kompassion – Weltprogram des Christentums: Soziale Verantwortung lernen*, Freiburg, Basle, Vienna.

Women's Voices and Feminist Theology: Accounts from Germany and the USA

HILLE HAKER, SUSAN ROSS AND MARIE-THERES WACKER

The state of feminist theology in Germany
(Marie-Theres Wacker)

Protestants and Catholics make up the vast majority of Christian groups in Germany. They represent about 52 million of an overall population of about 80 million. The next largest group is the Muslim faith with about 3.5 million registered members.[1] In contrast to the USA, other Christian groups like Orthodox, Old Catholics, Pentecostals, Baptists, Methodists, Mennonites etc. are still very much in the minority, and are not regarded as part of the mainstream. On the Catholic side, Elisabeth Schüssler Fiorenza left Germany in the late 1960s, and at that time only a few women, such as Iris Müller and Ida Raming fighting for women's ordination, dared to speak out against discrimination of women in the Church. Since the late 1970s, Protestant (mainly Lutheran) women have been very active in the feminist Christian movement. The first feminist investigations into questions with regard to women in the Bible came from Protestants like Elisabeth Moltmann Wendel (1980) and Luise Schottroff.

Some years later (1986), the foundation of the European Society of Women in Theological Research (ESWTR), an initiative by women of the World Council of Churches, co-opted some Catholic women like Catharina Halkes from the Netherlands. At the same time, Protestant women theologians such as Christa Mulack, Gerda Weiler and Elga Sorge were at the forefront of the Goddess movement in Germany. During the 1980s, many Protestant, and Catholic, women joined feminist Bible study or prayer groups, women who then in the 1990s wrote their dissertations or completed their habilitation.

The experience of feminist theologians in the academic context, however, was a very different one. On the Catholic side, a number of faculties, such as Tübingen, Würzburg, Freiburg, Bonn and Münster, were open to feminist theologians in the early days of the movement. In the early 1990s, two faculties, Bonn and Münster, even established chairs for women's studies in theology ('Theologische Frauenforschung'). Today, ten years later, with the ongoing privatization of German universities, the funding for these chairs turns out to be less secure than other theological disciplines. At least one can say that, in spite of significant scepticism on the side of the church officials with regard to feminist theology, Catholic women theologians today hold chairs in theological faculties and also within teacher training colleges. Some women explicitly distance themselves from feminism, but many of those who were rather reluctant at the beginning have found their way to adopt perspectives of 'inclusivity'.

On the Protestant side, there has been a certain reluctance in the faculties to appoint as professors women who are known as feminist theologians. In the meantime, however, there are several women professors whose self-understanding is feminist apart from those who are not that much interested in feminism or who openly reject it. On the other hand, the church structures are in support of feminist theology. In the 1990s, the Protestant Church of Germany (EKD) sponsored the founding of an institute for women's studies, the Frauen-Studien- and Bildungszentrum, and the Bavarian Protestant Church (Bayerische Landeskirche) even established a chair for feminist theology at Neuendettelsau. Many young women today are ordained pastors, not a small minority of them inspired by feminist theology. And there are three women Protestant bishops: Maria Jepsen in Hamburg, Bärbel von Wartenberg-Potter in Lübeck and Margot Käsmann in Hanover. In both major Christian churches, women are represented in positions of leadership to the highest level: there are diocesan chancellors ('Ordinariatsrätin') on the Catholic side, and on the Protestant side there are equivalents in the regional churches.

Feminist theology and ethics: a personal account (Hille Haker)

I still remember my first day as a student at the university of Tübingen. When I asked for permission to enrol for an additional programme of study in order to gain a degree in social work, the dean's response was striking: no, he said, you cannot do that. Theology will demand everything of a man ('Theologie erfordert den ganzen Mann').

At that time, in the early 1980s, quite a few women in Germany had started to study theology at degree level, whereas until then most female professionals were trained at a lower-level school than the 'full-scale' seminary. In addition to the prospect of becoming a teacher of religious education in the state school system in Germany, the Church had started a programme for lay theologians, male and female, to fill positions in parish work, hospital chaplaincy, adult education and prison work, and women were granted theological degrees at state universities. This openness towards women was partly due to the fact that there were fewer priests for parish work than were needed. On the other hand, it was common sense that the job prospects of lay theologians within the Church would improve. The Protestant churches had started to ordain women as pastors; the 'pastoral assistants' system' with a high-level university degree was partly the Catholic response to the liberalization of one of the two main Christian denominations in Germany.

There was great interest in studying theology at that time, emerging out of parish youth work, the peace movement and the environmental movement that had emerged within German civil society at the beginning of the 1980s. Hence, universities welcomed students who were highly motivated and who could have high expectations with respect to their professional position in the Church. Together with the decline of seminary students, this 'lay movement' changed the shape of the student body at theology faculties in Germany.

Feminist theology did not play a very big part at that time, although it was present, and was debated in Tübingen and in other theological faculties in Germany. There were initiatives and a colloquium organized by the female staff at Hans Küng's Ecumenical Institute in Tübingen (Bernadette Brooten had left but her work was discussed, Anne Jensen was a long-term staff member). The faculty had agreed to offer a lecture course each year to be given by a visiting professor, which was meant to fill the gap in courses and scholarship. Having become interested in this field, I went to Nijmegen to study feminist theology. When I returned to Germany, this time to Munich, there were hardly any traces of the lively academic discourse I had come to know in the Netherlands in all theological disciplines, and after a year I returned to Tübingen.

Within my own field of theological ethics, there was certainly a lack of discourse in Germany, regardless of how much scholars like Dietmar Mieth sympathized with the field of feminist and gender ethics.[2] In the 1990s German women theologians like Regina Ammicht-Quinn, Marianne Heimbach-Steins and Austrian theologian Christa Schnabl published books on feminist theological ethics and gender studies – delayed by the overall context of Catholic moral theology and social ethics.

In my own academic work, I am interested in feminist and gender studies concerning theories of subjectivity, identity and narrative, and also gender ethics in the sciences, namely bioethics. Here the relation between feminist theory and gender studies is open for discussion, given that many issues in bioethics concern women in their roles, positions and life-planning. But on the other hand, gender is a category that needs explicit reflection as a constructive factor in scientific research. Theological traditions relevant for moral theology and social ethics, such as the natural law tradition or specific Christian anthropology, are often applied with no attention to contemporary critique or reflection. However, since they seem to contradict feminist thinking and the insights of gender theories, they need to be discussed in light of these theories – and to be exposed to internal critique. Moreover, the emphasis on justice as a category of Christian social teaching can – and needs to – be spelled out with a view to 'gender justice' on a global level. Christian feminist ethics could even be a leading force in the critique of actual global economic developments, and could press for the realization of the political goals, particularly those spelled out in the Millennium Goals of the United Nations, which are especially sensitive to women's health standards.[3]

The situation of feminist theological ethics within the academy is not very encouraging: the outstanding feminist theological ethicist, Regina Ammicht-Quinn, was denied the *nihil obstat* in theology faculties for non-transparent reasons. Academic scholarship could not be established in coursework as one of the fields that needs to be taught regularly and where more research is needed. Feminist discourse is more or less ignored and absent in moral theology. There is no initiative for a graduate school, let alone for a centre for feminist theological ethics. And there are not many students who have the opportunity to study feminist ethics and gender studies, while in other disciplines a feminist approach has at least become part of the syllabus.

In spite of these institutional shortcomings and research gaps, I can see a genuine interest and concern on the part of young theology students in my field of ethics – with regard to their role within the Church, with writings concerning the role of women, but also with respect to scholarship in developmental psychology, philosophical ethics, and feminist and gender ethics in the sciences. The dissociation of church writings from academic work is more than striking: a natural law doctrine that repeats an anthropology to which most feminist theologians cannot subscribe, the understanding of sexual life and homosexuality, reproductive rights, marriage and the family, ignorance of the structural injustice towards women in private, socio-economic and political contexts, and, to repeat the title of a recent issue of *Concilium*, the betrayal of trust by ignoring and even backing sexual assaults against minors while denying women the right to introduce children into the public life of the Church – all these are issues waiting to be debated, to be reflected upon in thorough studies, in part to be sharply criticized from an ethical point of view, and, essentially, to be changed. The shift in the women's movement's debates, namely the disputes between feminism and gender theorists, between different kinds of a more contextualized feminist theology, crucial also for the further development of feminist theological ethics, has only barely reached Catholic theological faculties. The 2004 'Letter to the Bishops of the Catholic Church on the Collaboration of Men and Women in the Church and the World' rejects even open discussion of contemporary gender theory, and shows no respect for feminist scholarly work within theology. Academic theology, however, needs to address the questions of feminist theory and gender studies in order to gain a better understanding of our Christian faith. Neither feminist theory nor gender studies conflict as such with religious thinking or theology. Trust and curiosity, together with the commitment to our shared beliefs and the social and political responsibility to make the world a better place to live in, could pave the way for new scholarship in a field that has far too long been neglected in the German Catholic tradition.

Given the latest developments concerning appointments, but also the role of lay persons within the Catholic Church, the rejection of women's ordination and many things that have become standard in the German Protestant churches – are we today returning to the status quo of the early 1980s? As far as the academic establishment is concerned, I guess the answer would be yes. Whereas 25 years ago there was encouragement, a climate that something as strange as feminist theology should actually have a place in the university curriculum, I do not sense this today. Rather, the gap between academic scholarship, church policies and state indifference has widened. Women will be teachers. They will work in the traditional care and counselling professions, and hopefully will maintain their positions as professionals in parishes. However, highly educated women will be found less and less in permanent chairs in academia, or as directors of Catholic academies who play an important role for the German social culture of civil society, or as directors of institutes for adult education.

Women theologians, like their female colleagues in other departments of the German universities, who are the more in the minority the higher the academic rank (holding only between 4 and 7 per cent of permanent chairs), are more than ever dependent on the structural assistance and pressure of the university to appoint female professors or at least permanent lecturers. Whereas this pressure is used as a political instrument every now and then in the other departments, Catholic theology is 'spared' this state university pressure because of the state–church contract, which works to the disadvantage of women and female theologians. Hence, female professors in

Germany often enough enter their departments as the only woman, automatically being in the position of a radical minority. Furthermore, with the low prospects of the German theology faculties in general, not many lay theologians, female or male, will make it into permanent positions in the coming years.

Systematic theology and ethics: a personal account
(Susan A. Ross)

I began graduate school in theology after having spent three years working in business. I was certainly aware of feminism at the time, and was proud to be the assistant to the first woman vice-president in the investment company I worked for. But I was not very aware of feminism in theology. When I began my studies at the University of Chicago Divinity School in the fall of 1975, I was barely aware of the first Women's Ordination Conference in Detroit, even though one of my teachers, Anne Carr, attended it. I had felt empowered by Vatican II to study theology, and while I considered myself a feminist, I did not plan on studying feminist theology, in large part because the field barely existed and was just being developed. There were no courses in feminist theology at the University of Chicago.

In the winter of 1977, the Vatican issued its 'Declaration on the Admission of Women to the Ministerial Priesthood'. A group of students organized a discussion around the document, and I recall thinking at the time that the argument that women could not be ordained because we did not bear a 'natural resemblance to Christ' was ridiculous. That year, some of the women in the theology programme organized a women's group for reading, discussion and socializing, and it was there that I first became aware of feminist writing by women theologians. We began to develop a new awareness of theology through feminism. We invited scholars such as Rosemary Ruether and Phyllis Trible to come to speak to students at the Divinity School. A friend of mine lent me her copy of Mary Daly's *Gyn/Ecology*. After reading that book, my way of thinking was changed for ever.

For me and probably for many others of my generation, we learned feminist theology not in the classroom but in our own reading, after we had done the required reading that we had to do for our course work, and later on, after preparing for our own teaching. I completed my dissertation on the relationship between theologies of revelation and aesthetics, and it was only as I completed my final chapter that I realized that there were implications for feminist theology in my work: an understanding of revelation and truth not bound to linear thinking or to correspondence models of truth.

When I began my first teaching position in 1980, my new department chairperson assigned me to teach two sections of a required introductory course, and said I could do 'anything I wanted' for my third course. I chose to teach a course on 'Women and Religion', and then had to convince him that this was still 'systematic theology'. My undergraduate students expected a course in women saints and the Blessed Mother! We were inventing this field as we went along, sharing reading lists and teaching strategies. Since then, I have taught courses in Women and Religion, Gender and Values, and Feminist Theology at three Catholic universities for the last 26 years. Undergraduate students today are much more aware of what is involved in these courses, and are much more sophisticated in their expectations than were my first students. On the graduate level, there is interest in feminist theology among some students, but in many ways, feminist theology remains marginalized. Sister Jamie Phelps OP, an African-American theologian, describes the prevailing view of feminist, womanist and other liberation theologies as 'adjectival' theologies, meaning that they are not considered to be 'real' theology but a 'special kind' of theology that is done by and appeals to a small minority.

There is a community of women scholars in professional organizations and with my colleagues in other fields in the universities where I have taught. I first began attending the meetings of the Catholic Theological Society of America (CTSA) in 1982, and found other women with similar interests. We worked together in the continuing seminars of the society, and eventually helped to form the Women's Seminar in Constructive Theology of the CTSA. Elizabeth Johnson presented a draft of the work that eventually became *She Who Is* at a Women's Seminar in 1990, and the seminar continues to meet at the annual meeting of the CTSA. The combined meetings of the American Academy of Religion (AAR) and the Society of Biblical Literature (SBL) have large numbers of women scholars presenting in every field imaginable in religious and biblical studies, and their committees on the status of women have produced helpful mentoring and literature for women scholars at early stages of their careers. The Society of Christian Ethics (SCE) has an active women's caucus, which in recent years has pressed the society on such issues as sexual harassment and the ethics of family and dependant care. Many of us are active in the women's and gender studies programmes at our universities.

The current state of feminist theology in the USA

In recent years, I have been asked by a few book publishers whether or not feminist theology is 'dead', no longer relevant since it has made its point. Theologians and publishers can now move on to the next trendy issue. It is true that the initial energy and excitement of feminist theology's early years has decreased. Feminist theology is not a unitary field, and in the USA, womanist (African-American women), and *mujerista* (US Hispanic women) theologies have challenged (white) feminist theology for its failure to acknowledge the diversity of women's experiences. But feminist theologians continue to teach and write.

The situation in the USA is a mixed bag. We do not have the church–state issues that keep women out of university positions in European countries. Elisabeth Schüssler Fiorenza, Rosemary Radford Ruether and Elizabeth Johnson – all Roman Catholic – hold or have held endowed chairs at their institutions (some of them Catholic) and the numbers of women in faculty positions in theology and religious studies are increasing. Protestant women theologians hold full professorships at universities and seminaries. There are programmes in women's and/or gender studies at most colleges (undergraduate) and universities. Feminist women have been elected to the presidencies of the AAR, SBL, CTSA, the College Theology Society, and the SCE, and more of us are attaining senior rank. Yet at the graduate (master's and doctoral) levels, there are more and more conservative young men seeking graduate degrees in theology. For some graduate students, feminist issues are unknown or passé as they are more excited about radical orthodoxy. Required reading lists for doctoral comprehensive exams often have just a few token feminist authors, and students are likely to hear about feminist theology and ethics only in the classrooms of feminist faculty members. Young women graduate students wonder how they can combine family and career with little or no support from universities or government.

For Protestant women in the 'mainstream' denominations, ordination is open to them, and there are women bishops in the Episcopal, Lutheran and Methodist churches, as well as senior positions in other denominations. Women now constitute over one third of seminary students seeking ordination. Yet women still find it difficult to become senior pastors, and find it difficult to move out of associate or religious education positions. Ordination has not solved the problems of sexism. Roman Catholic women, who have served as pastoral coordinators for parishes, now find that new bishops are unwilling to place them in supervisory positions.

Feminist theology has found a place in the academy, but the real question in the USA is whether that place will be able to influence the larger sphere of academic theology and the church. Many women have become theologically educated and now constitute 80 per cent of the paid employees of the Catholic Church in the USA. Yet the Church's official teachings on women remain highly traditional. I find more cause for hope for women in the parishes and academic institutions than in official church teaching, since it is in these places that women have found places for their voices to be heard.

Notes

1. Bundesamt für Statistik, http://www.remid.de/remid_info_zahlen.htm (last visited: April 06), figures date from 2003, site updated February 2006.
2. Cf. *Tübinger Quartalschrift* and Ursula Konnertz/Hille Haker/Dietmar Mieth (eds), 2006, *Ethik, Geschlecht, Wissenschaft*, Paderborn: Mentis Verlag. See especially Mieth's essay in this book.
3. Cf. Human Development Report, 2005, http://hdr.undp.org/reports/global/2005/ (visited 22 March 2006).

III. Islam

Emerging Women's Movements in Muslim Communities in Germany

HAMIDEH MOHAGHEGHI

Women's issues in Islam are to this day a current and highly explosive topic. In the western world there are many who believe that due to the backwardness of Islam and its strict laws Muslim women are isolated, oppressed and imprisoned. This is confirmed through lack of authentic information, biased reporting in the media and reports about the inhuman circumstances of the lives of some Muslim women. This perception makes conversations difficult, particularly with those Muslim women who do not see themselves in the role in which they are seen. It is important to fight with all our strength and seriousness to improve the situations of those women who are oppressed by injustice and male domination. A perspective on how Muslims live and how we can understand their way of life which is objective and free from prejudice is necessary in order to be able to act in a practical and effective way.

There are no (stereo)typical Muslim women, although some try to find some of their representative characteristics. Islam communicates an ideal as to how human beings (men and women) are to live their lives; the social and actual realities do not always correspond to the ideal. Islam as it is practised is what human beings make of Islamic teaching, and that depends on regional cultures, traditions, political and economic realities.

'Islamic values' as understood by doctrine are hard to pin down. They vary from country to country and even within one country they can be very heterogeneous. In order to understand the attitudes and the way of life of a Muslim woman, it is essential to know about her traditional context and her particular understanding of Islam. Muslim women are individuals with a variety of different forms of life which are influenced by different elements.

To generalize about the way of life of individual women and to conclude that misogyny is inherent in Islam leads to prejudice from the start and makes an objective discussion very difficult. As a theologian involved in the 'Huda-Network for Muslim Women' I work on Islamic theology and women's issues. There are approximately 1.5 million Muslim women in Germany, predominantly of a Turkish background. Their activities depend on their level of education and their real opportunities. Meanwhile there are regional and some national women's organizations with different orientations. While educational institutions for women such as the ZIF (Centre for Islamic Women's Studies and Women's Relief) and the IPD (Institute for International Pedagogic and Didactics) focus on educating Muslim women, there are also regional informal organizations with an emphasis on Islamic teaching as a guide for everyday life. In their meetings women learn about the Islamic way of life and the practical application of Islamic teaching. Huda has a consultative function and publishes a journal in which theological and social issues are discussed. In some organizations there we can observe approaches to a reading of the Qur'an in its historical context and a critical engagement with the received traditions.

The lives of Muslim women in Germany are influenced by tradition, Islam and the West. The traditional and Islamic influences are communicated through education and are generally in accordance with the parents' understanding of Islam. Western influences and their dominance are experienced through day-to-day contact with society. In areas where there are different values there can be clashes. Women who live in the western world are partly under conflicting influences and are challenged to find their own position without surrendering their faith and their tradition. In a pluralistic society shared human values must serve as the basis for a common life. All involved have to be aware of opposite values. They are to be explained and understood in conversation. 'Being different' alone must not legitimate withdrawal from society. There are different forms of life which in a global society exist side by side. It is one of the challenges of our time to learn to live in the one society with people of different traditions and religions. We have to be able to experience mutual acceptance and respect.

Being a woman in a Muslim community

An Islamic community is a community of Muslims where faith can be experienced through the sharing of rites. Unlike in the Christian tradition, there is no institutionalized congregational life. Every mosque is open to all Muslims. There is no membership and no one is tied to any one mosque.[1]

Islam as a holistic religion knows of numerous ethical recommendations for all areas of life. Mutual respect and modest behaviour between men and women are important fundamental principles in the code of honour between the sexes. This codex, which is positive and supportive of dignified behaviour, wrongfully applied or overdone can lead to the exclusion of women from the public realm. In order to justify such behaviour, irrelevant arguments are used that are not part of Islamic teaching but the product of the human imagination. For example, in reply to the question why men and women pray in separate rooms or why if a shared room is used for prayer women are always confined to the rows at the back, one constantly hears from Muslims: 'so that men are not distracted by women when they are praying'. Here separate rooms are consolidated as a form of the encounter between women and men which is prescribed by Islam. While there is very little in the Qur'an itself with regard to a detailed code of behaviour, countless and very bizarre statements can be found about it in the traditions, for example in the so-called Hadiths. They go into great detail in prescribing the way human beings, and women in particular, are to behave in public. There are numerous traditions which literally try to justify the exclusion of women from society on the grounds of 'the laws of religion'. These traditions, however, ignore the early Islamic period when there was a very active interchange and fruitful collaboration between men and women. Their cooperation was free from strict and draconic obligations. During this time we know of women who passed on the teaching of Islam as teachers, theologians and legal scholars. Their role models were the wives of the Prophet Muhammad, his daughter Fatima and his granddaughter Zainab; their involvement in social and political affairs is significant. Their lives as persons of faith show that Islam does not want to exclude women from public life at all. In those days the place of women was not in the dark corners or the basement rooms of the mosque. They were not refused the right to voice their opinion or to express their questions and criticism in public. They were visibly present in society.

In Islam all human beings, men and women, are autonomous and it is their responsibility to shape their lives. Participation in the life of the community is not only a right but an obligation.

In order to do that everyone must have the opportunity to discover their own abilities, to develop them and to act accordingly. This requires unlimited access to resources in order to discover and explore one's own position and task and to shape one's own life individually in responsibility before God and the community. This understanding of Islam makes it difficult for Muslim women to cope with the actual traditions of some mosques where these prescribe a rigorous separation of the sexes and elevate these to being laws 'which must not be contradicted' which deny women active participation.

It must be said that separate spaces and activities are experienced differently by most Muslims. For many Muslim women spaces of their own represent safe spaces where they can shape their actions with other women without restriction. They do not see this as a disadvantage or as an obstacle to living an active life. The existing traditions which from the outside may be perceived as disadvantageous and as discrimination, seen from the inside have a variety of advantages which women like to make the most of and which they do not regard as a degradation. It is important to take into account these different perspectives in assessing the situation of Muslim women. The perspective from the outside can be useful for the termination of inequalities and oppression, but we must not expect that Muslim women will accept it uncritically and literally.

Western feminist movements have many successes to their name. Their engagement for women's equality in all areas cannot be denied. They deserve respect and recognition and can show the way forward in some areas. The question is whether it is possible for Muslim women to accept these movements uncritically with regard to their own emergence, and if they display a desirable success that can be a goal for all societies. The issues and the problem for the acceptance of western ideals and role models is aptly expressed in the following sentences:

> It cannot be denied that under Islam women have experienced much suffering as in the course of the centuries the rules of the Qur'an were interpreted more and more narrowly. Likewise customs and views which cannot be found in the Qur'an as such have become more and more rigid and have become tantamount to being canonical. Many things which are nowadays regarded as 'Islamic' are part of these more and more rigid layers. On the other hand we have to be careful not to see our ideas which originate from an 'unlimited' interpretation of the term 'freedom' as ideals for the whole world – and to dismiss customs and practices which we dislike as outmoded, even to condemn them. Muslims will easily understand the transfer of certain 'modern' ideals into the Islamic world as a new attempted colonization and it will thus provoke a strong counter-reaction.[2]

Globalization has made it inevitable that different cultures and religions will influence each other. The majority of Muslims are aware of the necessity to think differently and are prepared to make new attempts at 'enlightenment'. For this there are many approaches originating from the Islamic philosophical principles of the early Islamic period. They have to develop and to be shaped anew. Ways must be explored which correspond to Islamic theology, history and reality. In this way, the good and the bad experiences of others are able to teach us many things, but they are not for mere imitation or uncritical acceptance.

The revival of the tradition of Muslim philosophers such as Averroes (d. 1189), Avicanna (992–1050) and al-Kindi (ca. 800–870) can pave the way to an 'Islamic enlightenment'. None of them believed that faith and rational thinking were mutually exclusive.[3] Contemporary thinkers such as Abdolkarim Sorush and Muhammad Arkoun are examples of a new movement which is becoming more and more important.[4]

Identical terms – different interpretations

The differentiation between tradition and original Islamic teaching is gaining more and more significance; it is connected with uncertainties and the fear that the faith might become relativized. This development is particularly evident in the context of women's issues. The reading of the Qur'an and the tradition of the Prophet Muhammad is dominated by men who follow a patriarchal exegesis and try to justify discrimination against women through the Qur'an and the tradition (Hadith). Through education this way of thinking is communicated to women, so that they have a big problem in exercising and claiming the rights Islam grants them. It is extremely important to educate women with regard to these rights and to empower them to use religious arguments to resist the discriminations. Again and again in the course of history there have been women and men who have stood up for this. In this sense, enlightenment and movements of emancipation have a long tradition in Islam. However, time and time again they were rejected, twisted and badmouthed. In this context, the positive components within Islam are to be rediscovered again and again, they have to be considered in their context of time and space, they have to be worked out and fought for. Among other things this means to allow the tried and tested to stand and to make room for the new where it is good and useful.

In the Christian tradition one speaks of a feminist theology which, among other things, advocates a feminist reading of the holy Scriptures and women's access to ecclesial offices. Since in Islam there are no religious institutions and no administrative offices, appointment to such offices is not a topic of discussion. Traditionally mosques are rooms where prayers are said and where gatherings for the teaching and learning of religion take place. That women teach as theologians is taken for granted and has a long tradition. There are famous women theologians who had both male and female students. Khadija, Um Salama and Aisha, the wives of the Prophet Muhammad, his daughter Fatima and his granddaughter Zainab were the active Muslim women of the seventh and eighth centuries. They taught as women teachers and handed on the teachings of the Prophet Muhammad through traditions. Rabia of Basra is seen as the founder of Islamic mysticism. Numerous Muslim mystics were her pupils whose mystical teaching in turn influenced the works of later Muslim mystics.[5] Among the contemporary women theologians, Banu Amin (1895–1983, Iran) is to be mentioned. She achieved the scholarly grade of *hudjat al islam* and the permission to *idjtihad*, to practise law and pass a sentence in her own right. Her legacy comprises 15 volumes of Qur'anic exegesis and she taught several well-known Iranic scholars.[6]

Until fairly recently the question of whether a women could be an imam (prayer leader) was relatively insignificant. An imam is someone who leads the prayers of the community. The communal prayers for women can be led by a female leader. The prayers for men and for men and women together have traditionally only been led by a male imam. Until a year ago when Amina Wadud in New York led the Friday prayers for men and women, there had been no significant efforts on the part of women to change this tradition. On 18 March 2005 Amina Wadud, an Islamic scholar from Virginia, led the Friday prayers. This action triggered worldwide discussions among Muslims as to whether a woman could give the Friday sermon. While traditionalists held on to the view that this was impossible, there were also other voices who 'did not see being a woman as an obstacle to lead the prayers of the community'.[7] This action, however, did not trigger further movements as Muslim women did not see this as a crucial topic for discussion.

A 'feminist' theology as Muslims would understand it is a woman–centred interpretation of the Qur'an that would focus on the actual Qur'anic text and read it in its historical context. This means that the verses specific to women are to be read and understood in the light of the situation at the time and the position of women in the seventh century on the Arabian peninsula. As a result any literal reading of these verses for our time should be reconsidered. Such a reading should not lead to the faith being relativized. It should rather enable us to practise our faith in a conscious and contemporary way that can indeed be legitimized by the Qur'an and the basic principles of Islamic teaching. The question is therefore justified as to whether such a reading of the Qur'an calls into question the reading of the Qur'an as God's revelation in the literal sense.

This is obviously a very sensitive topic and arouses critical remarks on the part of scholars and traditionalists. Women participate more and more in this process of transformation and develop it further using the positive maxims in the Islamic sources. Such activities are not institutionalized and are intensified by the commitment of individual women. One of the women in Germany is Halima Krausen. As a theologian she has contributed a number of valuable publications and Qur'an interpretations on this topic.[8] Whether Muslim communities engage with and recognize the kind of reading mentioned above depends on the willingness of the respective communities to engage with new approaches and to accept them. It also depends on the women themselves and the perseverance and confidence they are willing to invest in their work.

Gender studies and gender theory are indeed being discussed among Muslim women. However, the development of the situation of women in the West, which is being perceived as a consequence of the women's movement of the recent decades, is being viewed critically. The problems of the West, such as high divorce rates, the destruction of marriage and family life, addiction, violence, indiscriminate sexual liberty, an increase in the number of single women without anyone to care for them, are seen as negative consequences of the modern theories and views. One suspects that they have created new problems rather than improved the situation of women. Women in the West still have to struggle with inequalities and injustices. These perceptions and observations confirm that women's liberation can be found in the Islamic sources which are free from patriarchal fictions.

Islam plays such an important part in daily life that one cannot ignore it but has to strengthen its positive potential. This approach is not in competition with all western values and achievements, nor does it defy them; it rather asks for an equal right to exist for a religion that has long become an important part of the western world. Muslims have a long and stony path ahead of them to grant women the right which Islam allows them. They are compatible with human rights; what is needed is 'enlightenment' in the most comprehensive sense of the word, to raise awareness of this compatibility. The improvement of the situation of women in the seventh century was the target of those Qur'anic statements that explicitly deal with women's issues. This aim always has to be in the foreground in order to be able to work out the necessary instructions for the implementation of this goal from Islamic teaching.

Conclusion

In Islam personal responsibility and decision-making are the basis for the shaping of the lives of individuals. One's own conscience and the use of reason play an important part; these challenge people to become aware of the real situation in which they live and to attempt to find possibilities for developing as a practising believer that are rational and realistic. This is a difficult endeavour in a work in which religion has little significance and is rather seen as an obstacle for progress and development. For me the critical challenge is the shaping of daily life, to be able to make a distinction between normative Islamic commandments and culturally and historically contingent laws. The conviction that Islam grants women the freedom to be active in all areas of life is not sufficient. The restrictions imposed on them by specific cultures and the laws of some Muslim societies de facto restrict women in their freedom to act. A public discussion about the abuse as well as reference to the positive factors in the Muslim way of life could lead to a corporate shaping of society. The current perception of Islam as the 'root of all evil' makes the necessary steps towards a trusting common life in western societies difficult and blocks the valuing of those elements of Islam that are worthy of recognition and from which these societies could benefit. The majority of Muslim women in Germany are active and wish to be taken seriously with regard to the whole of their way of life. They fight for more room to be active, particularly in religious institutions, and have achieved some successes that should not be disregarded.

Islamic identity is by no means incompatible with belonging to a secularized society; all involved should note and recognize this. Mutual trust and respect for the different forms of life in our society is the foundation for a peaceful life with each other.

Translated by Natalie K. Watson

Further reading

Lise J. Abid, 2001, *Journalistinnen im Tschador: Frauen und gesellschaftlicher Aufbruch im Iran*, Frankfurt: Brandes & Apsel.

Asma Barlas, 2002, *'Believing Women' in Islam*, Austin: Univ. of Texas Press.

Wolfgang Günter Lerch, 2002, *Denker des Propheten: Die Philosophie des Islam*, München: Patmos.

Banu Amin Modjtahida, 1970, *Makhzanul irfan dar tafsire qurane madjid* (Schatz der Mystik in der Interpretation des Qur'an), Teheran.

Ulrich Rudolph, 2004, *Islamische Philosophie: Von den Anfängen bis zur Gegenwart*, München: Beck.

Annemarie Schimmel, 1997, *My Soul Is a Woman: The Feminine in Islam*, New York and London.

Margaret Smith, 1997, *Rabi'a von Basra – 'Oh, mein Herr, Du genügst mir': Rabi'a von Basra und andere heilige Frauen im Islam*, Überlingen.

Karimah Katja Stauch, 2004, *Die Entwicklung einer islamischen Kultur in Deutschland: Eine empirische Untersuchung anhand von Frauenfragen*, Berlin: Weißensee Verlag.

Angelike Vauti (ed.), 1999, *Frauen in islamischen Welten: Eine Debatte zur Rolle der Frau in Gesellschaft, Politik und Religion*, Frankfurt: Brandes & Apsel.

Notes

1. In Germany there are 'Mosque associations' with registered members. These have developed in the specific context of the German legal system and are rather unusual for Muslims.

2. Annemarie Schimmel, 1995, *Meine Seele ist eine Frau: Das Weibliche im Islam*, Munich: Kösel, p. 185.

3. Ulrich Rudolph, 2004, *Islamische Philosophie: Von den Anfängen bis zur Gegenwart*, Munich: Beck

4. Wolfgang Günter Lerch, 2002, *Denker des Propheten: Die Philosophie des Islam*, Munich.

5. See for example Margaret Smith, 1997, *Rabi'a von Basra –'Oh, mein Herr, Du genügst mir': Rabi'a von Basra und andere heilige Frauen im Islam*, Überlingen; and Schimmel, 1995, *Meine Seele ist eine Frau*.

6. Modjtahida Banu Amin, 1970, *Makhzanul irgan dar tafsire qurane madjid* (*Treasures of the Mysticism of the Interpretation of the Qur'an*), Tehran.

7. Dr Mohsen Kadivar (a well-known Islamic scholar, head of the philosophical department of the teacher training college in Tehran and head of the NGO 'Freedom for the Press') replied in this context that he could not see a problem in women leading the joint prayers for men and women. If women are competent with regard to religious knowledge and respect the laws of Islam, he could not see a problem were they to preach and to lead the Friday prayers. He added that the widespread view that women's leadership of the Friday prayers was unacceptable did not originate from their faith but was rooted in outmoded traditions and cultures, in which women had always had a lesser role. Such thinking is not specific to Islam, it can also be found in other religions. He stressed that the time for revision of such thinking had come. From an interview with the BBC, 31 March 2005; see www.kadivar.com.

8. www.geocities.com/Athens/Thebes/8206/hkrausen/halhome.htm

My Father's Heir: The Journey of a Muslim Feminist

MEHRÉZIA LABIDI-MAÏZA

The core of my education was mediated through oral transmission of the Arab, Berber and Muslim memory of my family. My maternal grandmother, with whom I spent a large part of my childhood, made herself responsible for teaching me popular Islam, through her experience as a peasant woman as strong and as generous as her olive trees. From my father, the imam of our town, I received learned Islam, the version that embraces recitation of the Qur'an, the account of the life of Muhammad, messenger of God, and religious poetry and literature.

I see myself as a modern-age nomad, a '*mouhajira*' immigrant like the first Muslims, who set out for the four corners of the world bearing the most precious of treasures, their memory. How then should I describe my commitment as a woman other than by ransacking my nomad's memory, referring to my experience as a Muslim woman belonging to a generation that has witnessed the return of the Islamic religious presence on the social and political scene, with the resulting challenges? Speaking of my journey as a Muslim woman leads me to explain my – seemingly paradoxical – choice to practise my Muslim faith and to call myself a feminist, to repossess my Islamic religious heritage while opting for French citizenship.

Being born a girl into a practising Muslim family was more of an advantage for me, as my father was an enlightened religious man whose absolute priority was the education of all his children, five girls and three boys, on an equal footing. I grew up reconciled to my identity as a Muslim woman and even proud of it. On many occasions I heard my father defending his choice of education by invoking God's Messenger Muhammad, who was the father of four daughters and who promised eternal happiness to fathers who were benevolent with their daughters. In this way I came to love Muhammad and to listen to his message. The little girl that I was acquired an image of him as a farsighted father, an image often confused with that of my own farther, who was also named Muhammad – this father who was often criticized, not to say attacked, by those around him for 'the excessive freedom' he allowed his daughters. However, criticisms did not weaken his resolve to push us to the limits of our ability in our studies, inspired as he was by the Prophet and firmly convinced that a girl's greatest protection was and always would be Knowledge. He even laid down a rule that horrified my mother: not to accept a marriage proposal for any of his daughters until they had obtained their *baccalauréat*. This was how he saw the way to guarantee us our future and our autonomy. I have no idea how often my mother repeated that the most likely result of this rule would be to make her five girls 'old maids'.

I took up my studies like effective and priceless armour. I was curious about everything and especially driven to discover far-off lands through books. The Arabic, French and then English languages were my favourite subjects. By a happy chance, my language teachers were all women, French and Tunisian, who were very committed feminists. At the age of fifteen, thanks to my French teacher, I read *La cause des femmes* (*Women's Cause*), a pamphlet upholding women's rights to take control of their body and their life, written by the French lawyer Gisèle Halimi. This was my first discovery of 'feminism' as a social movement – a discovery made through books. As I grew older I realized that my second advantage was to have been born in a country where access to education was available to all without distinction of social class or gender.[1] If today I had to choose which measure to adopt in order to promote better conditions for women in a country where rights were being denied them, I should say without hesitation: access to education without caveats!

It was through my reading that I came to know feminism better, to appreciate certain aspects of it and to criticize others. For example, I did not feel at home with the aggressive feminism of Nawal Saadawi as expressed in her essays.[2] I confess I felt unable to understand the fury with which she denounced female circumcision and polygamy, since neither existed in my surroundings.[3] On the other hand, I greatly appreciated her works of fiction, which unmasked the hidden wounds of Arab women. I was already convinced that women are entitled to equality in human dignity, which should bring them the same freedoms and responsibilities accorded to men. The Qur'an is addressed to the whole human race, and it often states that men and women are partners and complementary; I believe religious men have distorted its original message by making women into eternal minors, dependent on men in their economic, social and even spiritual lives. Although I was a deep believer, I did not think that women's role was limited to their biological function, as certain religious works held. I was already refusing to read books justifying male tuition, imposed on women with the aim of protecting them, as though they were precious objects and not human beings. In this way, the emancipatory thrust of the feminist movement, claiming equality of rights between men and women and denouncing the discriminations imposed on the latter, has shown the way to all women who aspire to a more worthwhile existence. I therefore went along with this. But I found the attitude of most feminists excessive in their rejection of religion as an exclusively masculine and hostile institution, calling therefore for women who wish to gain their independence to reject their spirituality. In the wake of this, they go on to decry institutions dear to religion, such as maternity, marriage and the family. While I was and still am in favour of criticism and remodelling of these institutions, I am not in favour of rejecting them altogether.

I was very involved in feminism without yet being able to reject my Muslim feminine ideal, which I found in *Aïcha*, Muhammad's beloved young wife. I was – and still am – fascinated by her unrivalled personality. She preserved a large part of the prophetic tradition by memorizing it and handing it on to her contemporaries, who, in their turn, passed it down to successive generations of Muslims. She was in her way the heir to the Message of Islam, and she considered herself responsible for its safekeeping. So when Muslims complained to her about the social injustices they were undergoing at the hands of the Prophet's third Caliph,[4] she placed herself at the head of a popular opposition movement to denounce these. I was already seeing myself as a sort of combination between this model of Muslim womanhood and the contemporary model for women found through my reading. I saw no contradiction between the two!

Following the example of my Muslim heroine and drawing on this new model woman, I began to cherish an idea: I wanted to be heir to my father's memory and not be reduced to being 'the daughter of . . ., the sister of . . ., the wife of . . ..[5] I wanted be a person in her own right, capable of having a life project dependent on her and not on a third party, even if that were a husband. (I have, in fact, a husband who supports me and pushes me to carry out my projects.) I wanted in my turn to make sure of passing on that religion my father had instilled in me with so much love and openness. But I was forced to realize that my will came up against social taboos often confused with traditions, meaning religion. My father was in the habit of inviting 'pupils' of his together with friends of ours to discuss everything in general and religion in particular. He sometimes invited my sister, who was studying theology at Zitouna,[6] and myself to take part in these discussions. We realized that our contributions displeased certain of the guests. They thought that we were not in our proper place, there among men. Some of them even ceased coming to these meetings and to the talks my father gave at the mosque because he did not oblige his daughters – who should have set a good example – to wear the *hijab* (headscarf). This was during the early 1980s, when the religious revival was felt very keenly in Tunisian society, as in the whole of the Maghreb, thanks to the repercussions following the Iranian revolution. I shall never forget the lucidity and prescience with which my father invited the young men to temper their enthusiasm, assuring them during their discussions that women would be the first to challenge the lifestyle imposed by the Mullahs. I am grateful to him for not having imposed religion on my sister and me but for simply suggesting it and witnessing to it.

When, some years later, I informed my father of my decision to wear the *hijab*, he gently reminded me that my decision would sometimes make life in contemporary society difficult, adding that he hoped my choice sprang from deep spiritual conviction and not from infatuation with a fashion. This proved to be the case.

I have experienced three sorts of difficulty relating to the image projected by wearing the headscarf. They have taught me to be faithful to my convictions while negotiating good relations with those around me. This is not always easy! The two first difficulties came about in my native country. They came from the fact of wearing the headscarf being regarded as a political decision by those opposed to the Islamist political project but also by those who promote it. For the anti-Islamists, once a woman wears the headscarf, she is treated as 'a representative' of the Islamist political current, whether she wants to be or not. This can have serious consequences for the woman concerned, since she is automatically put in the category of people to fight. Freedom to believe, to practise her religion, or to dress as she feels she should all go out of the window.

The situation is no better with the Islamist partisans, as they tend to turn any woman wearing the headscarf into another voice to add to their cause. They believe that it is enough to declare in their speeches that Islam has liberated women for any practising Muslim woman to rally to their party, and for them to have a right to monitor her thoughts and her choice of way of life. One has to stand firm without confronting both extremes in order to exist as a woman who claims her right to practise her religion and to live her spirituality without being condemned by one or claimed by the other.

The third difficulty consists in the negative image of Muslim women generalized in the West. On arriving in France in 1986, I found this in the media, in people I mixed with at university, in interfaith discussion groups, in my neighbours. Once again I found myself classed among a category of women in which I could not recognize myself. My husband and I actually belong to that late wave of immigrants made up of students who chose to come to France to further their studies and their careers. I was not expecting to be lumped with those women who have very little or no education. Their religious culture is imbued with strongly patriarchal local traditions. They have suffered both a change of country and the xenophobia of the host society. Now they are suffering from the return to religion by their husbands, fathers and sons, who use it to make them feel guilty or to control them more strictly. The model they present to their daughters is not one I should like to follow.

My first reaction was to reject this image by concentrating on my own reality, but it did not take me long to realize that my life had nothing in common with that of the Muslim women who belonged to the first wave of immigrants[7] and their daughters, those who represent the majority of Muslim women living in France and even in Arab-Muslim countries. Through my participation in community-building activities with these women from the Maghreb and sub-Saharan Africa, I discovered their attachment to their religious values but also their confusion when faced with injustices done to them in the name of religion. The sincerity of their faith, their courage in the face of life's adversities and their reactions to injustice touched me deeply. Thanks to them, I came to understand that it was not enough to have a handful of educated and enlightened Muslim parents here and there who educate their children differently to bring about a change in the situation of millions of women who have to live in a precarious state made up of literalist and sclerotic readings of religious texts, made still more rigid by patriarchal traditions.

I moved out from my 'privileged' world in order to renew my commitment to my religion and to my feminism. I then realized the need to work with other women who were reconciled to their Muslim identity thanks to a positive religious education, so that together we could embark on a journey towards the repossession of our religious heritage in order to find our rightful place within Islam and within our respective societies – and to make other women eager to follow.

The way to 'repossession' of our religion as women leads initially through the capacity to ask the right questions. The first has to do with the very nature of the 'Muslim tradition' often invoked to uphold or justify unjust social practices that discriminate against women. This question was the starting point for all those – men and women – who have embarked on a reformist reading of the Muslim religion. So I found echoes of my own concerns in the writings of the philosopher Hassan Hanafi, who defines the Muslim religious inheritance as a dynamic notion: 'our inheritance is not a collection of rigid theoretical learning nor a body of immutable truths but the different embodiments and declensions of these theories and these truths at a certain time, in a certain group with its own view of the world.'[8] This definition of religious inheritance allows one to understand the diversity of – not to say contradictions among – norms called 'Islamic' that have regulated the status of Muslim women at different times and in different places. It thus helps us to see our place as Muslim women in relation to the Muslim tradition and to be capable of explaining it to those who regard it as a monolithic bloc. In fact the Muslim tradition is made up of the Qur'an, the Sunna (the prophetic tradition), the Fiqh (jurisprudence), the Madhahib (the legal schools) and the Sharia (the code that governs the various aspects of Muslim life), besides traditions and customs inherited from pre-Islamic periods, which have been Islamicized. Riffat Hassan, a contemporary Pakistani woman theologian, states that any attempt by women to redefine the Muslim tradition has to go through identification and analysis of its various components before daring to draw conclusions or to make generalizations.[9] A titanic undertaking! It cannot be carried out other than through multiple contributions by people with different specialities applied to a common aim: to give Muslim women their rightful place in their religion and their society.

Thanks to my work, I have been able to follow the progress of this undertaking in France. As a translator specializing in religious texts, I have often had occasion to work on the classic legal treatises dealing with the status of women.[10] This has enabled me to sort the wheat from the chaff in matters of religious prescriptions, traditions and customs. I have therefore been able to answer the questions of women I come across in the social centre or the neighbourhood associations by showing them what is from our religion and what is not. I have also taken part, also through translating religious texts, in some research projects concerning Islam and women, undertaken by academics such as Dr Mahbouba Merchaoui,[11] who dared to produce a critical reading of the 'Muslim tradition' concerning the place granted to women. She put the Muslim juridical and philosophical patrimony through the sieve of her feminine expert examination, questioning it on the role, views and conditions of women on both the spiritual and the juridical levels. This involvement enlightened me on the correlation between religious texts and their application in particular social situations. I became more and more interested in theology, and as I found different women's voices pleading for a Muslim theology with a woman's voice, I began to feel involved in their struggle and in sympathy with their arguments. Through the writings of Amina Wadud,[12] which examine the language of the Qur'an to demonstrate the impartiality with which it addresses men and women, and those of the Egyptian Amani Saleh,[13] that re-examine the creation accounts in the

Qur'an to show the original equality of both sexes, I have moved from the phase of questioning to that of working out answers. The contribution made by these women to the critique but also to the enrichment of Muslim thought has been a real message of hope for me.

By involving myself also in interfaith dialogue I have learned how to walk with other women: Muslim, Christian, Jewish, Buddhist – to serve the cause of all women, Muslim or not, and to provide a witness, of one sort or another, to our age. I have been able to keep abreast of the progress of Christian feminist theology and to appreciate our convergences and our differences.

These various encounters have helped me to work out my priorities as both a Muslim woman and a French citizen and to identify the advantages this situation affords me as well as the challenges it brings me. The first advantage lies in the possibility offered me by French society, in which freedom is a basic value, to express my spirituality and to individualize my religious observance while still maintaining a vital relationship with my community. The second comes from this multicultural and multireligious openness that allows me to meet other women from different backgrounds in order to build bridges together between our cultures and communities by drawing on our common femininity, not to say our feminism. It is also significant that the French feminist movement for equality includes many young Muslim women among its members.

Furthermore, I have been trying to forge links between women who are already involved in the production of Islamic religious discourse and struggling to enhance the image of Muslim women and those who frequent the neighbourhood associations, who continue to be oppressed by a religious discourse that is often distorted or warped by a rigorist or even fundamentalist interpretation. Meeting this challenge really matters to me deeply, as it now acts as a justification of my commitment as a religious woman and a feminist.

When I look back on my youthful dream of wanting to be 'my father's heir', I find that I am that, but with a few concessions to, or arrangements with, my surroundings, on the lines of the daughters of Zelophehad in the Bible (Num. 27 and 36), who made the case to Moses that they were the rightful heirs of their father, a request to which Moses responded favourably on condition that they choose husbands from among their cousins, meaning that they should stay in the group even if they had acquired new rights. I am concerned to keep the links with my community even if it does not evolve as I should like it to, in order to work for change from inside. I have inherited some peasant characteristics from my grandmother: I know how to persevere in my task with patience until the day comes when I see the fruits of my labour. In conclusion, I repeat my commitment to a feminist Muslim theology based on knowledge and expertise to enrich tradition and to promote women, not to create a 'matriarchal' reading on the lines of the 'patriarchal' reading created by men. My ideal is to have greater justice between Muslim men and women, a justice drawing on the initial equality between men and women enshrined in the Qur'an and reflecting the notion of solidarity and partnership needed between the two if they are to carry out their common task: to be God's representatives on earth.

Translated by Paul Burns.

Notes

1. Schooling in Tunisia was democratized and made compulsory for girls and boys following independence in 1956, in towns and rural areas, by the political will of president Habib Bourguiba.

2. A contemporary Egyptian feminist who has written some 27 works of essays, poetry and fiction.

3. The practice of female circumcision does not exist in the Maghreb, and polygamy was forbidden in 1956, thanks to the new Tunisian family code known as the 'Personal Statute'.

4. The Prophet's third Caliph, Uthman ibn Affan (Caliph from 644 to 656), had encountered strong popular opposition as a result of his laxity in matters of social justice. These disputes turned into a bloody conflict after Uthman's assassination (in 668), which led to the division of Muslims into Sunnis and Shias.

5. This is the usual way women are introduced in my circle.

6. The theology faculty is part of the university of Tunis and awards degrees from MAs in religious sciences to doctorates.

7. Those that came to France mostly after the law of 'family reunion' in 1972 to join their 'guest-worker' husbands.

8. Hassan Hanfi, 1984, *Al-tourath wal-tajidi* (*Patrimony and Reform*), Tunis; see especially the introduction, pp. 11–15. Hanafi is Egyptian and is one of the contemporary Muslim thinkers who have initiated the task of reforming Islamic thought.

9. R. Hassan, 'An Islamic Perspective', in Jeanne Becher (ed.), 1990, *Women, Religion and Sexuality: Studies of the Impact of Religious Teachings on Women*, Geneva, pp. 93–128.

10. Some examples: in 1994 I translated collections of fatwahs, concerning Muslim women, covering different concerns (from spirituality to political involvement) and different periods (from the first century of Islam to the present); in 1997 I

translated a higher education manual on the foundations of Muslim law; and in 2002 a sociological study of the contemporary Muslim family.

11. In 1993 Mahbouba Merchaoui gained a doctorate from the Paris X Nanterre University with her thesis, 'Femme musulmane, marginale des Oulémas, oubliée des philosophes'. Since 1995 she has taught philosophy at the Islamic University of Kuala-Lampur.

12. Amina Wadud, 1999, *Women and Qur'an: Rereading the Sacred Text from a Women's Perspective*, New York: Oxford University Press.

13. Co-founder of the Arabic and English review, *Women and Civilization*, published in Egypt since 2002.

IV. Hinduism

A Conversation on Two Faces of Hinduism and their Implication for Gender Discourse

MADHU KHANNA

Being a Hindu woman

I was born Hindu and brought up in a fairly devout family of followers of the god Vishnu-Krishna and his consort, Radha. An exploration of the nature of Hinduism and the diversity within it will help to clarify my location as a Hindu and a woman, and my thinking about gender questions.

Hinduism is the oldest living faith in the world. Its roots can be traced to prehistory. It is the religion of 70 per cent of the 700 million people of India. The Hindu tradition, while presenting several parallels to other great religions, cannot really be compared with them. Hinduism is not a religion of one book or a single prophet, but a process, a way of life where competing claims have found an honourable place. It is often acknowledged that 'nothing can be asserted about Hinduism that cannot also be refuted'. The word 'Hindu' has fairly fluid boundaries and no definite religious connotation can be attached to the word. Hindu is best understood as a 'culturally orientating term'. Traditional Hinduism works its way intrinsically through a decentralized structure; its distinguishing feature is its diverse form of religiosity that exists in innumerable combinations within its vast social fabric. The divergent viewpoints have been in some form or other 'approved, defended, prescribed and standardized' by often conflicting or contending sources of authority. In an old scripture, for example, a woman is described 'as a seed of the tree of life' in the first half of the verse; in the next 'a torch bearer who can lead a man to hell'.

This cultural diversity is traceable to four major streams of tradition that have converged to form Hinduism. First, there are the traditions of the numerous tribes and primal communities of *Adivasis*, who are the original inhabitants of India, historically traceable to half a million years ago; second, there are influences from the Indus civilization; third, there is the ancient Dravidian culture represented by Tamils; and finally, there is the Vedic religion, which came into India with the waves of Aryan invaders that spread all over the north of India. The encounter and contact with Muslims and the colonists contributed many ideas, but also disrupted and wiped out many age-old patterns. Nevertheless, the culture has endured.

A historical survey

The position of women in Indian culture has varied from age to age. In the oldest layers of our civilization, the Vedic period (2500 BCE–1500 BCE), religious ceremonies were open to women. The Vedic age produced a score of eminent female scholars, poets and teachers. Girls had the same status as boys and upper-caste women were entitled to *upanayana*, the sacred thread ceremony. Women, therefore, enjoyed a considerable degree of freedom in the early Vedic period of history.

By the pre-Buddhist period women were ineligible for Vedic studies. The neglect of education and lowering of the marriage age, together with the rise of asceticism, produced disastrous consequences for women. Illiterate child wives became the order of the day and women were often compelled to submit to unworthy partners.

In the orthodox Brahmanical male-defined culture of later periods, the birth of a son embodied a source of hope, while the birth of a daughter was a source of anxiety, tension and despair. The Vedic society preferred sons to daughters. Being born a daughter was a penalty for some sin committed. Female infanticide was not uncommon. The birth of a son was celebrated over that of a daughter because the sons were invested with the duty of ancestor worship that would ensure spiritual liberation for the parents. The sacred law codes also perpetuated sex-role stereotypes allowing for greater options and flexibility to the male child and imposing greater restrictions on girls, assigning them to only play the domestic roles of a wife or a mother. The secondary or inferior status accorded to the girl child resulted in the heinous crime of female feticide. By and large most references in our prescriptive literature show that the birth of a daughter was unwelcome.

In the male-dominated Hindu scriptures, derived from the experience of men and based on institutions dominated by them, the attitude towards women remained ambivalent. Women were not considered legitimate agents. They were considered to represent *maya*, or the illusionary power of their material world. Misogynist remarks and negative oppressive slogans extol women's lower status. In the Law Books women were lumped with sinners, slaves and outcastes. Later they were considered to be ineligible for performing religious rites.

In the orthodox Hindu view women came to be regarded as intrinsically evil, spiritually impure, poisoning by their very presence and constituting an impediment to salvation, thick of mind, poor of judgement. They represented a raging passion of lust since they were beings of insatiable sexual desire. This literature imputes to women shallow base natures, weak intellects and insatiably wanton desires to seduce men.

By the Epic period (400 CE) both the institution of marriage and its status as obligatory for women were well established. Women were perceived to be created for the sole purpose of producing male progeny and for a life of subordination and bondage to a husband who was regarded as a deity in human form. While the ideal of marriage was based on the complementarity of the male and female, the hierarchy of the male over the female was solidified. The wife's chief duty was full submission to her husband as a god. In this role she was described as a *pativrata*, as someone who obeys her husband.

The wife was given a status of auspiciousness (*mangala*) on account of her marital state. Her purity was reflected mainly through her fertility, prosperity and ability to produce male progeny. Although valued for her fertile powers, the attitude of orthodoxy remained oppressive. Traditionalists held that women were unclean, defiled and impure during menstruation. An overwhelming number of taboos were imposed on her to channel and control her sexuality.

Challenges and contradictions

Tragic or exhilarating, the Indian religious landscape as we have seen from the above discussion is permeated with multiple challenges and contradictions. The status and dignity that society accords to women is the true parameter for judging its strength and depth as a nation. Although Hindu religious philosophy symbolically conceived women as a reflection of a goddess, embodying multifold inner virtues and strengths endowed with divinity, technically known as Shakti, or Cosmic Energy, this idealization was not reflected in their status on the social plane. Customs of child marriage, *purdah* (the seclusion of women), *sati* (the practice of widows joining their dead husbands on the funeral pyre), restrictions on remarriage of widows, and property rights, pushed them further to adopt an inferior position.

The numerous reform movements in the nineteenth century, and the introduction of policies, laws and programmes for the social and moral uplifting of women, have enabled us to claim our rightful position. Reforms in the sacred laws mean that today we have the right to receive education, inherit our own property, cast a vote, participate in the public and political life of our nation, follow a chosen religious path, even worship a set of hybrid gods from different religions and lead independent lives. However, these supports are more open to elite women in urban areas who enjoy equal rights with men. Women in rural India still do not have access to all the institutional supports whereby they can assert their rights. We have now the Dowry Prohibition Act of 1961, Specific Relief Act, Common Law for Domestic Violence, Sexual Harassment at Workplace Bill, and the like. The policy for the empowerment of women instituted in 1991 aims to bring about the advancement of women in all spheres. Although the policy for women spells out 'full development', few women realize their 'full potential'. New policies must be addressed to the majority of women, not to a minority who live in urban India. The adoption of the western model of growth has effaced many levels of our cultural and religious identities with egalitarian-secular goals. Rural women, the Dalit, the tribal women and those who are on the lowest rung of the ladder – the invisible, unspoken and unnamed women – should also be receivers of the benefits of growth.

Gender studies and its critique

In recent years, most explorations in the field of gender and culture in India have been viewed from a Marxist, Socialist, liberal or modern perspective in the context of the socio-political reality of our society. These approaches have consigned cultural resources, such as religious scriptures and texts, symbols, powerful feminine icons in oral and written tradition, myths, and legends, the lifestyle of primal communities and grass-root traditions to the dust heap of history. In more cases, these cultural resources have been looked at from a western or alien perspective and have suffered from the onslaught of the reductive theoretical positions that modernity adopts to view ancient or different civilizational cultures.

Moreover, earlier epistemologies were based on the theoretical frameworks of western science. Some feminist scholars have brought out the inherent inadequacies of this approach to discuss the diversity and variety of experiences in the consciousness-raising sessions of women. The personal and collective oral histories of women have opened up new avenues for framing discourses of religion and their culture. Together with this, gender

studies programmes in South Asia have had to adopt innovative method-
ologies and interdisciplinary approaches to explore women's issues. Unfortunately, despite the progressive inclusion of research centres for Women's
Studies in Indian universities, a very large corpus of women's culture and
religious experience has remained outside the domain of academic scrutiny
and analysis. The thrust of research in these centres is based on theoretical
models from the West. Hence, while the institutionalization of gender
studies has opened many doors of speculation, their orientations tend to be
limited to the choices made on secular grounds as to what role a multifaceted
culture could play in re-visioning an indigenous form of feminism in India.
Therefore there is no institutionalization of feminist (Hindu) theology in the
Indian context.

Despite the opportunities for gender studies in India, feminist research
on the role of religion, in women's culture and their indigenous knowledge
systems, suffers from neglect. It is to fulfil this need that a first attempt of
its kind has been made in launching Narivada: Gender, Culture and
Civilization Network, a programme under the aegis of the Indira Gandhi
National Centre for the Arts, India's premier national institution engaged
in the preservation and dissemination of knowledge in the fields of arts,
culture, lifestyle studies and folklore. This was launched in 2005. From its
inception, this programme was concerned with creating a new vantage point
of looking for our past by taking a constructive rather than only a critical
view of civilization resources.[1]

Leadership (of women) in Hindu traditions

In the political sphere, the first step that enabled women to play leadership
roles at the grass-roots level was taken when India passed laws that make it
mandatory for local governments to include women in the governance
process. Therefore, since 1993–94, one third of the seats in local bodies are
'reserved' for women. The law unleashed an opportunity for leadership and
local governance.

In the social sphere, there is considerable participation of women at the
grass roots who lead self-help groups, day-care centres and women's centres.
Some feminist critics have pointed out that such activities of leadership,
while giving some opportunity to women, create 'an illusion of emancipatory change' while the patriarchal institutions are kept in place!

In the religio-spiritual domain, women's leadership patterns vary considerably in relation to the contexts in which they appear. Religion plays an
inextricable role in people's lives in India. A larger component of the

population of women in India can be safely placed in a generic category of
'religious women'. In India, religion is not predominantly a male enterprise.
Women play active and conspicuous roles in the religious life in the domestic sphere, although they are invisible socially. Most Hindu women across
India have some kind of religious life of their own, even where they conform
to male ideals of womanhood. In both the domestic and public sphere, a
man's and a woman's religious life are distinguishable. There are innumerable domestic rituals for the attainment of fortune and prosperity that are
exclusive to women. The religious world of women is rich, vital and diverse.
These women may not fit into the category of religious leaders in the public
domains, but they wield the power of auspiciousness (*mangala*) and
beneficence, valued dearly in Hindu society. The married woman is symbolically looked upon as a goddess Lakshmi, since she extends the virtues
of purity and good fortune. In the role of a mother the religious woman is
considered to be a 'leader' of the family.

In contrast to the more familiar and popular participation of women in the
religious sphere, there have been a fair number of women of 'extraordinary
callings' whose contribution to Hindu religion and society has been well
recognized. Beginning from the *brahmavadinis*, Gargi and Maitre, of the
Upanishadic period (1500 BCE), down to new-age female saints and gurus in
India such as Ananda Mayi Ma, Sharda Ma, the wife of Ramakrishna, Mata
Amritananda Mayi, Her Holiness Madhobi Ma, and many other women
who have responded to an extraordinary calling, we find massive support
and social and political recognition of them as religious leaders. These
women break out of the mould of institutionalized religion, and tend to
transcend the orthodox roles assigned to them. Once accepted, they subvert
the norm. Some of these women leaders are renunciates; others combine
their spirituality with the domestic roles of wives and mothers. On the
whole, the religious woman in India finds support, where her religious role
is validated by the codes of Law specified to women. Yet there are also
women leaders supported by the political Hindu groups or the Hindu Right-
Wing fundamentalists, who are distinguished by their obsessively Hindutva
activism, and cultivate violence exploiting a militant identity.

The central question for scholars of religion and culture

The most obvious question for the scholar of religion is to explore the
multidimensional contexts and diverse identities of women. There is a great
need to create a new hermeneutics of gender discourse where the questions
are framed taking into account our multiple cultural and non-cultural iden-

tities of women. The thrust of scholars until now has been to view the women's question in the context of two major categories, the hegemonies of caste and class that form the hierarchical structures in our society. Thus the gender question should be framed in its totality, taking into account diverse contexts (rural, urban, tribal), and women's multiple identities. Several crucial areas from the vast resources of Indian heritage have been air-brushed from history by the secular feminists. These areas need to be re-interpreted and recognized by scholars of religion and culture.

Counterculture

Hindu culture is more than the sum of its orthodox texts. We have to view the textual tradition as the backdrop for cultural processes that move society in altered directions to change the dominant paradigms which once domi-nated society. Scholars of religion in India are beginning to acknowledge that religion is among the foremost of institutions that conserve society, by encoding orderly world views and value systems that are transmitted from generation to generation. Religion is equally significant as an agent of change and social transformation, which encodes, re-codes and reframes a plethora of radical views unleashing the potential of human creativity.

First, there are a vast number of resources in our written and oral heri-tage, emerging from the treasury of dissenting traditions such as the Tantric traditions, that revalidate a pro-women ethos. This pro-women ethos runs counter to the orthodox tradition. Alongside these relatively well-organized pockets, several Hindu ideas from the Sanskritic tradition intersect, or run parallel to, the traditions of 360 primal/tribal communities/groups and the folk traditions of the rural people who live in India's 500,000 villages, dis-tributed in different parts of the country and composed of different races and cultures. It is in these little-known, under-researched, parallel sub-streams of culture that one can discern a radical and liberating construction of gender. These traditions consciously or unconsciously have abandoned almost all orthodox concepts of caste, class and subordination of the female or her bodily functions. The affirmation of the power of women is actualized in innumerable forms of casteless worship, where women of all ages and social class received worship. Women have autonomy and authority in public spheres. They can play (and have played) powerful religious roles in society. They have religious choices to become priestesses and gurus, initi-ate disciples, run ashrams and hold autonomous positions in the religious life. This is a dramatic shift in a culture where women by and large are not allowed to play such roles.

The second resource, the rich and vibrant goddess heritage of India, is crucially important for the recognition of the authority of female power. The Indian Goddess is primal and perennial and her representations, running into thousands, if not millions, form the gynocentric core of Indian culture and civilization. There are goddesses who are spouseless, without male . partners, or adoring spouses in close embrace with their male partners, maiden goddesses, heroines, saintly and erotic figures, comely and terrible, creative and destructive personas; nature deities who protect land and habitat, goddesses who bestow grace and compassion and those who proffer beneficence, emerging from the Sanskritic as well as village-based traditions. The unbroken history and proliferation of goddesses, and the absolute supremacy of some goddesses (such as Durga, Kali, Tripurasundari, Alli) stand in direct opposition to the western view that maleness is the norm. The female-centredness of the Hindu world challenges the notion that maleness is the primary form of human experience or even a measure of human values. Feminist scholars pursuing a serious study of religion and gender should bring out the inadequacies of a non-sacred goddessless 'secular' view of the world and expose the cognitive imperialism of the secularists' pseudo-claims to universal truths and impersonal reality. Although this is a contested view, I believe that the goddess tradition provides one of the richest resources for our liberation.

The third resource that has great potential for shaping and strengthening the argument for an indigenous discourse on feminism comes from the oral or 'intangible' heritage of women. Women have preserved a large number of traditional knowledge systems. Firmly grounded in religious revelations they have drawn inspiration from folklore, epics and age-old models of virtuosity. And it is these resources that deserve scrutiny.

All these three resources, whether they emerge from dissenting traditions, goddess traditions, or from oral regional sources, can be examined for a new assertion and restoring of the dignity of personhood.

The contexts and frames of our discourse

How and where do we position the role of Hinduism and gender? The indigenist framework presupposes an understanding of the multicultural matrix of our culture, and the distinctiveness of our contexts. Modernity in such a system will have a special location but not the advantage of superimposing its own mindsets and value regimes. Cultural pluralism is intrinsic to India. Multiculturalism by definition means a resistance to a singular monolithic world-view: respect for difference, celebration of the regional, the local, and the oral versus the written. Plural cultures of which India is a prime example are essentially hybrid, fluid and latently ambiguous, or even doubly coded. Such cultures give space to the 'other' to redefine their identities in their own terms. The essential nature of this polytheistic culture is to further pluralism and to overcome the elitism of the establishment. They are naturally open systems and can never exhaust the agenda of growing world-views. In this cultural matrix, convention and liberalism are continuous and mutually enhancing. India's sub-culture's relation to the conventional mainstream is so constructed that while shunning and discrediting it, it has also offered several profound alternatives. Hinduism's unorthodox heresies such as the Tantric and Agamic traditions, the bhakti traditions, region-specific orally based rural and tribal traditions, and the voice of the subaltern majority have carried out hidden conversations among lineages, between conventional and liberal religious groups. These contesting views have existed side by side. It is in these sources that the indigenist framework for gender and religion must be redefined.

Note

1. For more information, see www.ignca.nic.in/narivada.htm.

Affirmation of Self:
A Hindu Woman's Journey

LINA GUPTA

'The *Divine Mother* exists in everything, animate and inanimate, in the form of power or energy. It is that power that sustains us through our lives and ultimately guides us to our respective destination,' quotes Swarupa Ghose, a housewife with a newborn baby in her lap. She is one of the many devotees participating in the Autumn Festival of the goddesses, the major festival of the Hindus in Bengal, an eastern state of India. Her comment echoes the sentiment and the faith of the majority of Hindus.

Three reasons motivated this paper: first, my Hindu upbringing and my long-term research work on the goddess tradition motivates me to share with others my experiences and reflections in the area of Hindu feminism. Second, the women I interviewed on my trips to India wished me to be the voice for their responses to the western analysis and negative stereotyping of Asian women, especially Hindu women. Third, my recent research experiences of the Autumn Festival of the goddesses in India prompted me to investigate the status of Hindu women from a different perspective.

My personal journey

My writings as an ecofeminist have been an exploration of goddesses as the divine feminine, the manner in which they manifest themselves in the human female and the options they present as possibilities, actual and otherwise, for fulfilment as a feminist. The journey, however, was not a simple one.

My upbringing and training in Hinduism, to my satisfaction, facilitated any aspirations I've had as a philosopher and as a feminist. My understanding of Hinduism has been enhanced by these aspirations. Two incidents, occurring fifteen years apart, marked a radical shift in my academic direction.

In the late eighties, I was invited to participate in a conference on the goddess tradition at Claremont University. I was rather baffled by the invitation to be a presenter on a topic relating to the goddess tradition because my academic focus had been completely on the monistic aspects of Hinduism which deal with the concept of divine as a nameless, formless, state of being that transcends all forms of categories and characterizations. This neutral state of being, however, manifests itself in infinite forms. I logically understood that in its essence, Hinduism is monistic and most devotees accept the idea that often for the sake of human concentration we need tools such as images and idols which are merely the pointer we retain until we internalize the essence of the Ultimate Reality. All three facets of Hinduism, polytheistic, monotheistic, monistic, made perfect theoretical as well as practical sense to me. Yet initially, I was not willing to shift my academic focus from monism to polytheism, or even to monotheism for that matter. Humility, however, provided the impetus for my transformation into an ecofeminist, a transformation that occurred literally overnight. I experienced the divine in an entirely different form or manifestation. I was, in a sense, a witness to my own birth as an ecofeminist and champion of Hindu goddesses. The experience was both participatory and one in which I existed as an audience member to myself.

To my surprise, I eventually began to note another form of dissatisfaction. My years of academic affairs in the West had left me abandoned and feeling disconnected from my Hindu identity, aching to revisit and reclaim my Hindu identity. The opportunity came in the form of a Fulbright grant to do research on the Hindu goddesses in India. With trepidation I arrived in India shortly before the Autumn Festival. The entire state was buzzing with activities, from building numerous temporary festival sites, making the images, building new roads, information booths, temporary police stations, first aid and rescue centres, all in anticipation of the holy days. Although this was the place of my childhood, I began to view the phases of the festivals, from the making of the images to their immersion in the Ganges, differently after having been away for some time. Thus I became both a participant and a witness, yet again.

The Hindu notion of creation, preservation and destruction is a self-generating cyclical notion without separation, and this became quite evident in my search for my roots. As a Hindu woman and feminist, I have come full circle. Some things need to be lost in order to be found. My faith permitted the realization of my self relative to my Hindu centre. Even when I feared that I had lost this centre, and that it had been destroyed by my distance from its source of power, other aspects of my life and self allowed me to see that this part of me actually had never been misplaced or forgotten.

A critique of western feminism

My research focus shifted from the celebration to the celebrators themselves, primarily the female participants who are integral to all aspects of this celebration. My subsequent academic work became not only an echo of their voices, but also served as a vehicle to relate their journeys as individuals. It is to honour these voices that I must proceed.

I have found, in conversations, in articles and in other media, that some western feminists feel it necessary to label Hindu women of the East as oppressed (forgetting that such labelling is itself a form of oppression). Although perhaps well intentioned, this kind of description creates an ambience of imperialism. Intrusive disregard for Hindu women's persons, their opinions and their cultural concerns is hardly conducive to healing and smacks of patriarchalism. It is well to remember that absolute power and oppression function culturally. It is quite difficult to remove the context of our own beliefs and opinions which bias our interviews of these women.

Feminism is saturated with the idea that males fear the feminine, and that it is manifested as a belittling of anything that resembles female traits. One must wonder whether western feminists' assessment of eastern women's 'oppression' is a subtle transference of that same fearful sentiment which western feminists are so attuned to in their own struggle(s). We have learned that oppression has many faces, appearing in disguises both subtle and obvious. Women in the West, however prosperous and educated they may be, are not exempt from these realities.

International encounters such as at conferences have repeatedly shown a pattern of angst/frustration with regard to feeling categorized and misrepresented by their western sisters who exaggerate and contextualize an observed norm. Some of this friction is from the current opinion that non-American women are often illiterate, and for this reason, justify feminists speaking as educated women on their behalf.

The purpose of this paper is twofold: to be an echo of the Hindu women's voices, and honour those voices. From homeless to prostitute, matriarch to housewife to the professional, they are the visage of their inner strength and witnesses to their own struggles.

It is essential for a feminist to acknowledge the whole and not merely the individual fragments. Enough has been discussed and written on the subject of the patriarchal mindset as one of the reasons behind the ambiguities displayed in various traditions in their treatment/mistreatment of women. It is necessary now to identify what are the sources of strength and power in

Hindu women. For it is precisely this that has sustained these women in the face of their triumphs as well as their tragedies.

It is quite difficult to make a legitimate generalization about a society as complex and as heterogeneous as India. Hindu women are not part of a monolithic group. Their concerns and issues vary from community to community and region to region in various states of India. My analysis is not intended to be a definitive statement about Hindu faith, rather it is meant to illustrate a dominant mode in the wide and variable range of Hindu thoughts and behaviour.

Contemporary women's experiences

Worship of the Great Goddess in her many forms is enduring and widespread in India. However, it is in the North East of India, and specifically in Bengal, where the full-fledged autumnal celebrations of three major goddesses, Durga, Kali and Laksmi continue with their joyous celebrations of ancient practices and forms. In addition, Bengal has maintained a rich, dynamic and unbroken tradition of powerful goddesses that inspires and empowers women in their local milieu. The many facets of feminine experience, issues and solutions are reflected in the myriad of myths and rituals in various Hindu texts.[1]

In Bengal, the four-day Durga *Puja* or worship turns into a carnival when all other activities seem to stop and everything comes to a standstill till the devotees, satiated with festivity, finally reluctantly return to work. Streets are rigorously cleaned, temporary worship sites are erected in honour of the mother goddess, and corners are heavy with traffic and commerce as they sell merchandise in honour of the deity. Artisans are busy sculpting the images with clay collected from the river Ganges, a goddess in the Hindu tradition. Morning till night, all generations, classes and ages visit, offer flowers and candles, and make their rounds of the temples with surreal joy. This celebration highlights the merging of the sacred space and time with the individual and divine. The festival reflects the sacredness of an otherwise ordinary piece of land and a statue and the fine line between the sacred and the profane. Neither power inequalities nor any gender discrimination is evident during the celebration. On the contrary, the gender dynamics and communal involvement are significant as both men and women from all castes, classes, even from other traditions, gather to celebrate the holy days. The dominant theme in this celebration is the empowerment that permeates the celebration from preparation of the clay image to its immersion in the river, from the performers to the observers, from the priests to the devotees.

The primary focus at the Autumn Festival centres on the mother goddess Durga, the warrior goddess. She is often portrayed with ten hands, each of which holds a different object or ammunition, and she is seated on a lion. Surrounded by her four children, two of which are Laksmi, goddess of prosperity, and Sarswati, goddess of knowledge, she arrives at her birthplace, the earth, to save the planet from the wrath of the demon, who threatens the stability of creation. Initially she appears to be a traditional, married woman with four children. A closer look reveals her dual nature: with one she conquers life-threatening situations and with the other she maintains her home and hearth. She is a wife, a mother, a woman, but mostly she is beyond any form of characterization. A modern woman very well could identify her multi-tasking ability with her ten hands. The objects she holds in her hands reflect the measures she takes in facing her life.

In my interviews, I encountered women from all walks of life, from housewives to professionals, homeless to wealthy matriarchs surrounded by maids and servants, and prostitutes to conservatives. What binds this diverse group of women is their faith in their respective tradition and their inner strength gained through their practices. The following comments echo the sentiments of the members with regard to devotion and divine empowerment, the very core of Hinduism. The more the women identified and named their experiences, the more attuned they became to their inner strength and their faith community.

The comments made by numerous Hindu women offer us a clearer picture of how they perceive themselves, the Goddess, and the connection between the two. Most significantly the comments offer us an insight into their feminine identity as well as to their religious identity.

'The stories relating to the gods and goddesses enlighten me in human affairs in a significant manner, and offer me a code of behaviour, a standard that we could follow' (Susoma Bose, a high school student).

'Within the context of Hinduism it is not just the women who are barred from performing the actual ritual, men are too. It is not gender-based, rather caste-based. Only the male brahmin priests are allowed to perform the ritual' (Dr Maya Sen, a feminist historian and the head of a local girl's high school).

'These temporary worship grounds become a gathering place where we often forget other issues and concerns at least for the few days of the celebration' (Soma Dasi, maid of a wealthy household).

'The strength I experience during these holy days sustains me throughout the year. We all eagerly wait for the mother goddess to return next year, we all do' (Kanchan, a prostitute I interviewed in the red-light district in Calcutta).

'Power is not necessarily what we experience in our social and professional status. It has also much to do with what I feel inwardly. Divine mother is reflected in me, as such; power is in me' (Manju Kar, a grandmother).

'The more I am involved in image-making, I realize the symbolic meanings of the various aspects of the deities' (Seva Ghose, an artisan who heads the two-hundred-year-old family business of image making).

'The most interesting thing about Ma Durga's look is the expression on her face. The expression in her glaring eyes is that of anger, but her face is ever smiling. The total expression that comes across is that of an indulgent anger. There is Ma Durga in every woman. Durga's trinayan, or the third eye, present in every woman, helps her to see things beneath their surface and gives her a special power of understanding (Sarbari Dutta, a designer).[2]

'The uniqueness in the concept of Durga is that instead of bestowing her great power on a male God and sending him off to battle, Durga performs her own heroic exploits with the help of an army of female deities' (Rita Das Gupta, also a designer).

'In the villages of Bengal, the married daughters customarily came to visit the parents during the Durgapuja. Devi Durga assumes the parental role and we greet her every year as daughters. Yet her image – with ten hands holding different weapons and the posture on the lion, with formidable demon slain at her feet – reminds us of the Goddess who destroys all negativity, ego, passion, anger, desire, delusion and hate' (Supriya Sen, a college professor).

'Durga and Mahishasura as aspects of our nature are relevant even today. Both internally and externally, we face constant strife in the world around us, our home or our own selves, we are not the joyous beings that we can be. In the combined form of Durga, Saraswati, Lakshmi and the Shakti represent different aspects of energy which are manifest within us. But the demon Mahishasura is also manifest within us' (observes Bansari Lahiri, a Sanskrit scholar).

'I come from a community of Saraswat Brahmins where women have equal rights with men. We worship Durga as *shakti* (power). I do feel that if you communicate with the Almighty strongly she comes to your rescue. The ambience has a lot to do with this. The sound of *dhak* (drums) beats, the scent of *dhuno* (incense) and the chant build up an atmosphere where you get into a trance, literally or metaphysically' (Kalpana Lazmi, film-maker on Durga as a symbol of women's emancipation).[3]

Each one of these goddesses, Durga, Laksmi, Sarswati, is responsible for bringing either inner or outer balance. With one hand each goddess blesses her devotees. Her support, strength and wisdom are necessary for survival. As stated in the news, 'truly empowered women come in all shapes, sizes, all dresses'.[4] It wasn't until I interviewed other women and documented their responses that I understood what it meant to be Hindu.

Major concepts

The concept in Hinduism which has shaped my personal journey is the openness and freedom it offers to its followers. Religion is understood as a personal journey as well as a communal journey. Ultimately it is up to the individual to pursue the goal as she/he understands it. The choices Hinduism offers to its followers are evident in the concept of the divine, the ways to self-realization, and the respect it shows other traditions. One is free to conceive of the divine according to one's preferences and desires, be it the divine feminine, masculine or the non-dual transcendence, called the Brahman.

One is also free to choose a path of self-realization specific to one's temperament, preferences, and mental/physical capacities. Textual guidelines on the paths, such as knowledge, action, devotion and meditation, are merely suggestions. Differences among human beings call for differences in paths and the means people must take to reach their ultimate goal.

This openness leads to the notion of nonviolence, the key concept in Hindu philosophy. Nonviolence is not a passive act, rather an active search for dialogue and consensus based upon the idea that in honouring others, we honour ourselves. In nonviolence, we understand that many apparently conflicting judgements are possible about anything and that each judgement gives only a partial truth, but everything has multiple aspects. In meeting and dealing with others in our social relationships, tolerance is usually evidenced in a couple of ways: we either view others as unique and thereby hold their being as sacred to ourselves as our own being, or we become indifferent and detached and trivialize their being, often reducing them to the status of things. To reject others and to claim one's own path to be the only way simply defies the very notion of the divine being infinite. Even the most conservative Hindu accepts other faiths as various ways to the same goal.

Conclusion

As with many creative literary endeavours, this article has not only grown out of my professional interest in ecofeminism, but is also a chronicle of my own journey. It is a journey into my Indian background, my Hindu heritage; most importantly it is a journey into a memorable past, to my origin, and into a future, to my end. I wonder whether all settlers in the West must necessarily grapple with this process of discovery, however difficult or professionally disconcerting the experience may be. At some point in one's chosen path, facing a crossroad of life, self-analysis becomes inevitable. One wonders how much is left behind and how much of one's origin has been forgotten, and in which direction lies the future. In one's journey one learns to paint a single unitary picture of wholeness with the hues from both the Hindu heritage as well as the western experience of the present.

Notes

1. This essay draws significantly from my previous work in 'Kali the Savior' in P. M. Cooly, W. R. Eakin and J. B. McDaniel (eds), 1991, *After Patriarchy: Feminist Transformations of the World Religions*, 1991, Maryknoll, NY: Orbis Books, pp. 15–38; and 'Ganga: Purity, Pollution, and Hinduism', in Carol J. Adams (ed.), 1994, *Ecofeminism and the Sacred*, New York: Continuum, pp. 99–116.
2. *Times of India*, 11 October 2002, p. 1.
3. *Calcutta Times*, 15 October 2002, p. 1.
4. *Times of India*, 31 October 2004.

V. Buddhism

Gender Equality, Buddhism and Korean Society

YOUNG-MI KIM

Buddhism and the Korean tradition

Buddhism was introduced into Korea in the fourth century CE from China. Korea was then divided into three kingdoms: Koguryo, Paekje and Silla. Buddhism was accepted with the support of the state, and its influence on the lives of Koreans was equal to that of Shamanism and Confucianism, which were the predominant religions in Korean society. The evidence of this influence is found in the murals of ancient tombs of Koguryeo such as the First Tomb at Jangcheon or Muyong Tomb, which show the procession and worship of monks and believers or the picture of magnificent lotuses, which is the symbol of Buddhism. Other remains that reflect the influence of Buddhism are many images of Buddha carved into stone found in the Southern Mounts of Kyeongju. These pictures and sculptures indicate that Buddhism was an important part of Korean culture. Buddhism also changed the Koreans' thinking on life and death. As they learned about Buddhist theories such as the Cycle of Existence (reincarnation) and the Universal Law of Cause and Effect (Karma), they began to wish to be reborn in paradise (Pure Land of Utmost Bliss) or as human beings, instead of as beasts or demons. Henceforth, Buddhism became one of the major currents that motivated traditional society on the Korean peninsula.

The age that saw the peak of Buddhist culture, with the utmost patronage of the state, was the Koryeo period (918–1392 CE). Every year many rituals including Yeondunghoe (meetings with Buddhist lanterns) and Palgwanhoe (meetings to observe the eight commandments) were held at temples and the palace. The complete Collection of Buddhist Sutras, carved on eighty thousand wooden blocks, was made as a means of defending the country against the invasion of Mongols. The enormous amount of work invested in this collection shows how much the people of Koryeo depended on and respected Buddhism. There are also a number of Buddhist paintings and Sutras written in gold or silver that suggest the generosity of Buddhist believers.

At the end of the Koryeo period, leadership positions in society were taken over by Neo-Confucianists. Critical of the corruption caused by Buddhism, they did not allow women to enter a temple, except for the purpose of performing ceremonies for ancestors. After establishing the Chosun dynasty (1392–1910 CE), Buddhists were persecuted by Neo-Confucianists and an attempt was made to establish a Neo-Confucianist society. Men who wished to enter the bureaucratic order had to study Confucianism and were gradually estranged from Buddhism. Ceremonies for one's ancestors and all other household rituals were formed after the Neo-Confucian norm, *Chu Ja Ka Rye* (Zhu xi's principles for the home). As a further means of oppression, the government also issued an edict forbidding people to visit Buddhist temples. While men obeyed it, women did not stop worshipping at temples. This led the state to enact an additional law that prescribed 'flogging a hundred times for visits to a temple'. It is worth noting that women did not compromise their faith in spite of this additional law. And this tendency carries on until today: women believers make up 70 to 80 per cent of the Buddhist population, and half the members of the Jogye Order – the largest Buddhist Order in Korea – are *bhiksuni*, Buddhist nuns.[1]

Not until after the 1980s, however, was there an active movement to understand and practise Buddhism from a feminist perspective. As their labour participation and thus their social power had increased, Korean women gave their voices to the feminist movement. Other significant factors that gave rise to the Buddhist women's movement are, first, Koreans' increasing interests in the social status of women, which had been given increased attention since the International Women's Year of 1975, promoted by the United Nations, and, second, the nascent form of Buddhism which shows less gender discrimination than in the present. In 1985 the national nuns' association was reorganized and began regular activities. In 1990 the Korea Women's Buddhism Union Association (*sic*!) was formed, and in 2000 the Buddhist Women's Development Institute was established within the Jogye Order. In particular, I would want to note the Buddhist Women's Development Institute's attempts to create a Buddhist culture based on gender equality.

The lives of women in Korean society and in the Buddhist faith

The most important traditional values of Korean society, originating from Confucianism and Buddhism, demanded of women three types of obedience: towards their fathers during childhood, towards their husbands during married life, and towards their sons after the death of the husband.[2] It was taken for granted that once a woman had reached a certain age she would get married. Being unable to have a job and participate in social activities, the range of women's work was within the home. The esteemed women of Koryeo times, therefore, are exemplified in Lady In. The wife of Kim Won Ui in the period of Koryeo, Lady In was a fervent Buddhist, and devoted herself to reading the *Kumkang Sutra* (*Vajracchedika-Prajnaparamita Sutra*) before her marriage. She was outstanding in her filial piety and her love for her siblings was great. After being married, she obediently kept all norms of decorum required of her in her relations with her parents-in-law, and was indeed respectful and contributed to the peace in her husband's household. In her treatment of slaves and concubines she was merciful and dignified; she was strict but not cruel, which led them to fear her but not dislike her.[3]

Filial piety, companionship and ability to run a household by presiding over slaves were among the important assets of a woman. Another virtue required of women of the times was good management of the house, even in cases where the husband did not look after the economy of the home. Women, in place of their husbands in the governmental offices, needed to be responsible for the home economy and management. Women, the sole partakers of the household chores, had their concerns limited to the family, and the family's comfort and prosperity were their only aspiration.

This domestic role of women lives on to this day. Even in today's Korean society, where women's social advancement is admitted, women are expected to undertake all work within the home, from duties associated with filial piety to the rearing and educating of children. While the male role has the financial responsibility to support his family, a woman's activities are still restricted to the sphere of the household. The social activities considered appropriate for women are mostly related to their children's education.[4] The centre of the woman's world is her family, and she works hard to accomplish her husband's financial and social success, send her children to prestigious schools, and let them find a good job after their education is finished.

The faith of Buddhist women has a strong link with such social status of women. The strongest motivation for Korean women's faith in Buddhism appears to be their desire for their family members to prosper in society. In

Korea the social success of children is largely related to the universities from which they graduate, so one of women's main religious activities is to pray for them to go to good schools. It is a common phenomenon for every temple around the country, especially 100 days before the university admission examination day, to be filled with people praying for their children to get into desirable schools. Christian churches are not exceptions regarding this occasion. Another important aspect of women's Buddhist faith is to pray for their dead family members to be born into paradise.

This aspect of women's faith is also revealed in their religious practice on the Buddha's birthday and the Buddhist All Souls Day. A vast number of believers gather on the Buddha's birthday, and light lanterns in Buddhist temples. Every lantern has a name of each family member, and has the effect of prayer for blessing. They also light white lanterns praying for the happiness of dead family members in the afterlife. The All Souls Day, another popular Buddhist occasion, is a day to pray for dead family members to be in paradise. The days designated for Buddha's enlightenment and death are also important memorial days, but cannot compete with the above-mentioned two days in the number of believers that gather for each occasion.

However, not all women practise the Buddhist faith almost solely for their family. Women who are usually tied down with housework become able to participate in Buddhist festivals as members of society. The believers of each temple are found to be mostly female, and women therefore organize believers' unions and support Buddhist temples and religious festivals. Through such opportunities, women are fulfilling their capacity as members of society. They can also freely travel with people other than their families, by taking part in pilgrimages to holy sites. A lot of women are also driven to the practice of Buddhism as a means to overcome the pains of life. The teachings of Buddhism state that 'all beings of this world change, and not one stays the same; not one entity remains still'. Women believers experience this teaching within their lives, and because obsession with hopes for unchanging and fixed entities makes life painful, they practise the methods of Buddhism – meditation, prayer and sutra chanting – in order to overcome such obsession and advance towards enlightenment.

Such activities of faith could help elevate the quality of life for women believers, and to this day are important reasons for women believing in Buddhism.

The life and status of Buddhist nuns

It is an important Buddhist tradition that men and women leave home for more active discipline, shave their heads and become monks and nuns.[5] But in traditional Koryeo society, those who wanted to be ordained needed the permission of the government. Illegal monks and nuns certainly existed, and the government imposed a strong ban on women leaving home to become nuns. This ban is specifically related to the dominance of Neo-Confucianism, which, with its ideological emphasis on women's purity, only allowed widows to leave home for the purpose of preserving their chastity. And this policy continued into the Chosun period, banning unmarried women, who had no dead husbands for whom to preserve their chastity.

According to the value system conferred upon women by the society at that time, a woman could leave home only after her marriage, the death of her husband, and her children's reaching adulthood. The Buddhist faith also emphasized the roles of women as daughter, wife and mother, as did the Neo-Confucianists. Except for female orphans who left home because of poverty, it was only possible for a woman to leave home after her husband died and her children grew up. This meant that they tended to become ordained very late, compared to men who could leave before the age of 15.

The practice of being ordained for the purpose of chastity has recently disappeared. As the social status of women improves, many highly educated women are ordained before or without getting married, to practise Buddhist discipline.

Let us take a look at the procedure to become a nun, and the status of a Buddhist nun, in the context of the Jogye Order, the largest in Korea. In order to become a nun, six months of education as an ascetic is required, after which the female Buddhist novice is given the status of ascetic (female Buddhist novice). Next a standard education of four years must be taken in one of the regular educational institutions such as the Buddhist Studies division at Dongguk University or Joongang Sunggha (Buddhist monk) University. Upon completion of this course, the graduate is given the complete precepts of a monk or a nun, which signifies an official qualification as a Buddhist monk or nun. At Dongguk University and Joongang Sunggha University nuns are given modern advanced education, and at monks' colleges and Seon monasteries they gather apart from the monks to learn the sutra and practise the Seon meditation. At present, monks' colleges for nuns include the Donghak temple (located at Gongju, Choongnam), Bongnyung temple (at Suwon, Kyonggido), Uhnmun temple (at Chungdo, Kyungbuk). In addition, around forty Seon monasteries are located around the country.

Of all of these places, the monks' college for nuns at the Donghak temple was established first, in 1956. The monks' college at the Uhnmun temple has the largest number of nuns. At these monks' colleges, subjects for more advanced education such as foreign languages are taught in addition to Buddhist sutras.

According to a survey carried out in 2004, there are 1,398 female Buddhist novices (and 1,814 male Buddhist novices) and 4,673 nuns (and 4,646 monks), making a total of 6,071. Looking at the total number of men and women that have left home to become ordained, some 51 per cent of them are men. However, it is worth noting that there are more nuns than monks. Comparing with 1999, when there were 6,245 males (including both male Buddhist novices and monks) and 5,728 females (including both female Buddhist novices and nuns), we can notice that there is a larger increase in the number of nuns than of monks.

This increase in the total number of nuns has led to an increase in nuns entrusted with work at organizations responsible for the administrative duties for the Jogye Order, such as at its headquarters and council. There are 35 Buddhist priests who are entrusted with such duties as high-ranking heads and directors at the headquarters of the Jogye Order, and 5 of them are nuns. Also, 10 of the 81 council members are nuns. These figures certainly do not reflect the large percentage of nuns in the Order, but they connote a great increase compared to 10 years ago; the number of council members in 2006 is twice the number of nun council members of 10 years ago. Not only that, nuns engage in active social work and are prominent in missionary work with children and youths, as well as the management of social welfare institutions. Nuns responsible for Buddhist research and leadership of the educational system at universities and monks' colleges are also on the increase. However, problems of gender discrimination still pose a challenge for the Order, one example being the Eight Commands, which obligate a nun, be she old or young, to bow first before a monk, be he older or younger than she.

On the other hand, some nuns actively commit themselves to reconciliation and communication with other religions. Samsohoe was established for such a purpose, and is an organization of religious women of Korea. The organization began with a music recital, which was held in 1988, in order to help disabled people. It has encompassed, up until now, women believers of Catholic, Buddhist, Won Buddhist, and the Episcopalian faith. One meditation and prayer meeting is held every month, and in 2006 there will be pilgrimages to holy sites, beginning with the Won Buddhism holy land in Korea, carrying on to India, Jerusalem and the Vatican. The organization has held meetings with religious leaders including dalai lamas, Muslim imams, as well as Catholics and Protestants. Through such dialogues the organization acknowledges the belief that all religions are about realizing peace in the world and serves to convey this truth to the public.

Women's enlightenment: two conflicting viewpoints

Whereas Buddhism liberated women to some extent, it also had the effect of suppressing women's activity in Buddhism. Some Buddhist orders and monks claimed that it was impossible for a woman to be enlightened, just because she was female. This was due to the Theory of Five Obstacles and Theory of Transforming into Men, first developed in the first century BCE and well known in the Koryeo society. The Theory of Five Obstacles states that women cannot become Wheel Turning Sage King, Heavenly King, King Mara, Brahman Heaven King or Dharma King of the Three Realms, who is identified as Buddha. These passages appear in the *Chepaldapum* section (*Devadatta Chapter*) from the *Lotus Sutra*, and the *Obunyul* among others. The Theory of Transforming into Men is about a story that the Dragon Girl turned into a man and achieved enlightenment in the *Chepaldapum* section in the *Lotus Sutra*. These texts indicate that a woman cannot become a Buddha.

Specifically in the case of Korea, the *Lotus Sutra* was considered important by the late-Koryeo Cheontae School, and therefore was used and read frequently; among others, *Beobhwa Yeongheomjeon* was compiled and distributed, and the subsequent propagation of the Theory of Five Obstacles and Theory of Transforming into Men signified a considerable influence of those theories on the people. Additionally, the monks of those times emphasized that it was rarely possible for women to be reincarnated as men, even if they had done many good deeds. This teaching contributed to the opinion that women must do a vast number of good deeds in order to be transmigrated, or transfigured into men, and furthermore that women needed to be men in order to become enlightened. As a result, there were some women who wished to be turned into men and be enlightened.[6]

On the other hand, the National Preceptor Chingak Hyesim (1178–1234) of the Seon[7] Order insisted that women can achieve enlightenment right at this moment, urging women believers and nuns to refrain from focusing on images of gender; in other words, to stop worrying about the fact that they are women, and instead to achieve enlightenment in haste. Consequently his female disciples practised for their own enlightenment, not just focusing on the bliss in the present world and paradise after death.

What was the reason for this difference between the monks' views on the possibility of a woman's enlightenment? In reality it was difficult for women to leave home to be ordained before getting married; after marriage a woman had to wait until after the death of her husband and the adulthood of her children. It was inevitable for orders that emphasized long-term discipline to exclude women from the possibility of becoming enlightened. In contrast, Seon monks were not assumed to need to train for a long time, and therefore were more open to women in terms of enlightenment.

The Buddhist monks' two different perspectives on women's enlightenment have been carried on until today. It is worth noting that the negative point of view on women acted as an important element in restricting women's activities, and limiting their religious activities mostly to pursuing the welfare and happiness of their families rather than their own enlightenment.

However, after the 1980s, Buddhist monks and believers started to realize that the original teaching of Buddha was based on gender equality. This change has made it possible for women believers to participate in meditation retreats of temples, which had been an opportunity for lay men to fulfil enlightenment but forbidden to women. Furthermore, women's activities, as well as those of nuns, are on the increase. Reflecting such tendencies, the Yonghwa temple at Inchon saw the development of a meditation hall for women believers, and the Buddhist Women's Development Institute was established.

The Bodhisattva meditation hall at the Yonghwa temple was developed in 1984, and allows women believers to practise, as do the monks, their retreat in the summer and winter for 90 days respectively. This meditation hall provides women with a place for enlightenment and the practice of Buddhism, and reflects the generally accepted idea that being female is not an obstacle to achieving enlightenment.

The main activities of the Buddhist Women's Development Institute include holding regular seminars for the purpose of empowering the women believers' sense of identity, and also for constructing the theoretical basis for Buddhist women's studies. Another important work of the Institute is to publish books to educate the public regarding Buddhist women's studies not only nationwide but also globally. It also runs a women's leadership programme for training Buddhist women leaders and a network for professional career women who wish to serve their society. A gender equality education programme is also available for monks and staff of the Jogye Order's headquarters, which seeks to help motivate women believers' religious activities. It also engages in a movement of cooperation with

Catholic and Protestant Christians, to facilitate social change for the better. One main example of such changes would be participation in the 'Religious Women's Union for Abolition of Head of Family Law' in order to nullify the Head of Family law, which restricted the status of women in Korean society. Recently, the Institute has started to focus on social problems stemming from a *low* birth rate and an ageing society, by creating the 'Civic union against *low* birth rate and ageing society' together with the Family Rehabilitation Committee of the Christian Council of Korea and the Committee for Family Pastoral Ministry of the Catholic Bishops' Conference of Korea. This is an attempt to resolve social problems through talks and cooperation between different religions.

Further reading

Hae Ju Cheon, 1999, 'The Present Condition and Direction of Buddhist Nuns in Korea', *Jong Gyo Gyo Yuk Hak Yeon Gu* 8, pp. 325–42 (in Korean).

Hanmaum Seonwon (ed.), 2004, *2004 International Conference: Korean Nuns within the Context of East Asian Buddhist Traditions*, Seoul: Hanmaum Seonwon.

Seong Hyo Min, 2002, 'The Status and Role of Korean Women Buddhists', *The Buddhist Review* 2/2, pp. 96–117 (in Korean).

Ki Woon Lee, 2001, 'The Establishment of Jeongeobwon and the Practice of Buddhism', *Jong Gyo Yeon Gu* 25, pp. 155–74. (in Korean).

Lewis R. Lancaster and C. S. Yu (eds), 1991, *Introduction of Buddhism to Korea*, Berkeley: Asian Humanities Press.

Young-Mi Kim, 1997, 'The Acceptance of Buddhism and Change in a Woman's Life and Awareness', *Yeok Sa Kyo Yuk* 62, pp. 37–70 (in Korean).

Young-Mi Kim, 1999, 'A Study on the Women's Entering the Buddhist Priest in Koryo Dynasty', *Ewha Sa Hak Yeon Gu* 25/26, pp. 49–74 (in Korean).

Young-Mi Kim, 2002, 'A Study on the Activities and Social Status of Buddhist Nuns in the Koryeo Dynasty', *Korean Cultural Studies*, Korea Cultural Research Institute, Ewha Womans University 1, pp. 67–96 (in Korean).

Notes

1. In 1972 some nuns established the Bomun Order of Korean Buddhism, which still exists today.

2. The Buddhist *Daejidoron* differs in that it suggests both parents, rather than only the father.

3. Gyubo Lee, 'The Grave of Lady In, Wife of Kim Won Ui', in Yong Sun Kim (ed.), 1993, *Koryeo Myojimyoung Jipseong [The Collection of Inscription of Koryeo]*, Chuncheon: Institute of Asia Culture Studies of Hallym University, p. 392.

4. According to a survey carried out in 2003 (Sang Lok Seo, 2005, *Women's Life Seen through Statistics*, The Department of Statistics), approximately 91.4 per

cent of married women replied that they are responsible for the rearing of children and household chores, regardless of them having sources of income. Of those women 39.6 per cent replied that they are solely responsible for housework whereas their husband worked for income; 33.6 per cent replied that they are responsible for housework even though both they and their husbands worked for income; and only 4.2 per cent replied that both they and their husbands worked and shared the housework between the couple.

5. Shaving their heads is an important process in the Buddhist ordination ceremony.

6. In 1346, Lady Cheon (the Esteemed Wife of Keum San Kun), donating for the image of the Medicine Buddha, prayed that she would further help humankind and that her female body be turned into a man's. This prayer was found in the statue of Medicine Buddha at Jangok Temple. Ki Baek Lee (ed.), 1993, *Hankook Sangdae Komunseo Jaryo Jipseong [The Collection of Ancient Documents of Korea]*, 2nd edn, Seoul: Il Ji Sa, p. 180. This concept had its roots in the *Medicine Buddha Sutra* (T. 14, p. 401c). According to this sutra, the Medicine Buddha made a pledge that every woman who heard the name of the Medicine Buddha be transformed into a man.

   Similar views are identified in the 1353 written prayer on the *Lotus Sutra*. In it was the wish to change the body into that of a man, in order to be enlightened. ('The Epilogue of the Lotus Sutra, written out in silver on navy blue paper', in Ki Baek Lee (ed.), 1993, pp. 208–9.

7. The equivalent of *Zen* in Japanese, and *Chan* in China.

Being a North American Buddhist Woman: Reflections of a Feminist Pioneer

RITA M. GROSS

In this informal essay, I would like to reflect on some of my key experiences and insights as a North American Buddhist woman and scholar-practitioner. How did I become a Buddhist in the first place? What was it like thirty years ago to be both a Buddhist and a feminist? Why do I think that Buddhists still need to be feminists? What has been most important to me about being a Buddhist? I would also like to reflect on what I have always considered the most important topic for Buddhist women – the presence of women teachers.

One may well wonder, given Buddhism's dismal record on equity and equality for women, why a western woman already well grounded in feminism[1] would choose to become a Buddhist. Indeed, after I began serious Buddhist practice in 1976 and took refuge in the Three Jewels[2] in 1977, most of my feminist friends and colleagues were totally mystified. They could understand Jewish and Christian feminists who would decide to work for change within their inherited traditions, but they could not understand why someone would convert to a foreign tradition not known for its support of women's equality.

My involvement with Buddhism actually began much earlier. I first began to study Buddhism as a graduate student at the University of Chicago in 1965, but did not find its doctrines very compelling. It was not that I disagreed with those doctrines. I was just trying to learn a lot about a lot of religions, fast, and to learn Sanskrit at the same time. Buddhism as a doctrinal system did not stand out. Nevertheless, I had been extremely taken by what I had learned of *Tantra* in my graduate school classes, and read everything available at that time on *Tantra* and Tibetan religions. They somehow made a deep impression on me, and, years later, I found that the stories that had drawn me the most were precisely the stories of the Tibetan lineages with which I had the most 'karmic[3] affinity' and whose practices I later took up with great enthusiasm.

In the meanwhile, feminist issues were of much greater importance to me. I had always been keenly aware of the subservient position of women in western religions and had quietly rebelled and tried to work for change. As I moved further into my doctoral studies, I became aware of the pervasive androcentric (male-centred) methodology of my chosen field of study, which always thought of men as the more interesting and only important subjects of research. It may be hard to believe now (at the time of writing, in 2005), when there is so much research about women and religion, but only forty years ago there was no information about women's participation in religion in any of the major sources and the topic was completely 'off limits'. I was told that studying women was unnecessary because men were already being studied and 'the generic masculine includes the feminine, making it unnecessary to focus specifically on women'.[4] Given how pervasive gender roles are in most traditional cultures and the sexual segregation so characteristic of most, it still baffles me how learned scholars could have made such uninformed deductions, but such was the conventional wisdom of those times.

Buddhism caught up with me in the fall of 1973. I was teaching a college-level survey course on Buddhism for the second time, struggling to understand its basic doctrines more adequately. I was also extremely unhappy. I had just moved to Eau Claire, Wisconsin, where I have now lived for more than thirty years, and had quickly realized it was going to be a very lonely place for me. I was also mourning the terminal illness of my lover, whom I had seen for what I knew would be the last time just days earlier. As I walked to my class on a beautiful fall day, trying to better understand the Four Noble Truths, which I was about to teach, I only longed to be able to appreciate the beauty of that day unburdened by my misery. Suddenly things became very clear. I could not appreciate the beauty of my immediate surroundings because I so desperately wanted things I could not have. Buddhism's second Noble Truth, that desire is the cause of suffering, became completely clear. I did not need to be convinced of the first noble truth, that suffering pervades conventional life. But the third Noble Truth, that suffering ceases when its cause – attachment – is given up also became utterly clear in a vivid instant of complete detachment and openness. I stood still and said to myself, 'The Four Noble Truths are true!' Unlike most academics, who might hold ideas philosophically without taking their practical consequences to heart, I immediately thought that if the first three truths were actually true, then the fourth truth, which details Buddhism's specific path, must also be true. That would mean that I should learn to meditate, something not easily accomplished in northern Wisconsin in 1973.

I did find a way to learn to meditate, and several years later, in 1977, I finally found my way to one of the major centres for Buddhism in North

America – Boulder, Colorado – to receive deeper training in meditation. I had decided before I left Wisconsin that, while meditation was valuable, I would not become a Buddhist. The main reason was that I had already been through two sexist religions (Christianity and Judaism) and didn't need a third trip through a religion that preferred men to women and limited women severely. So what happened? I can only say that the experience of living in a Buddhist environment thoroughly captivated me. I remember crying as I decided that Buddhism was simply too profound to let the patriarchs have it without protest. But I went into Buddhism with my eyes wide open. I knew that taking refuge in the Three Jewels meant that I would also be writing *Buddhism after Patriarchy*.[5]

It was not easy then, nor is it especially easy now, to be both a Buddhist and a feminist. The North American feminist theological establishment is not especially attuned to issues concerning religious diversity, despite its sensitivity to cultural diversity within Christianity. Many seem to believe that a white North American cannot authentically be a Buddhist, a viewpoint my Tibetan woman teacher scorns. They hold this viewpoint even while asserting that Africans and Asians who have become Christians are simply exercising religious choice. Buddhists generally are no more sympathetic to feminism. Many North American Buddhists, having little knowledge of Buddhist history or of Asian Buddhism, deny that Buddhism has any patriarchal baggage, citing the usual naive claim, 'I've never been discriminated against.' To them, somehow this claim seems to prove that, therefore, male dominance has never existed in the past or the present. In addition, Buddhists have problems with 'causes', especially when they are voiced in an aggressive manner that suggests self-clinging and attachment. However, issues of equity for women and women's equality are especially avoided. Even the engaged Buddhist movement, which self-consciously takes up contemporary political, economic and social issues, almost never concerns itself with gender analysis or women's issues.

Sometimes people try to corner me into declaring a primary loyalty. But to me, the Buddhist way of hyphenating its most profound wordings about reality solves that dilemma. Rather than prioritizing deep insights, Buddhists usually claim that, though different, they are of equal value. Thus, we talk of the inseparability of form and emptiness as emptiness-luminosity. Neither word by itself really captures what Buddhists say about the ultimate nature of our experience, and both are necessary. But the hyphen makes them, in a sense, one word. I would say the same of Buddhism-feminism. When both are properly understood, there can be no hostility or division between them.

Having taught and written about Buddhism so much for so many years, it is difficult to pinpoint exactly what about Buddhism makes me so committed and enthusiastic. It would be easy to say, as do so many western Buddhists, that Buddhist meditation practices are what makes Buddhism so appealing. A meditation practice involving silent sitting for considerable periods of time was the completely new ingredient in our lives. Early on, it *was* meditation that made all the difference. It had a profound effect on me in only a few years, making my rage over sexist injustice unworkable.[6] But one doesn't really have to be a Buddhist to practise the basic discipline of mindfulness-awareness, or *samatha* meditation. Many Christians also practise that form of meditation, which was common in India before the Buddha's time.

In the long run, what brings joy to me and what keeps me in Buddhist orbit is what is unique to Buddhism – *vipashyana*. This term is impossible to translate accurately, though 'special insight' is a common translation. For most people, Special Insight does not occur without the formal meditation practice of *samatha*, without the many types of mindfulness-awareness practice, but Special Insight is not limited to times of formal meditation. The experience that first turned me to Buddhism was an experience of Special Insight, a penetrating and clarifying breakthrough to a different level of understanding. For me, a verbal person, those experiences cry out to be put into words, but the path of Special Insight is always beyond words and concepts, which is not to say that verbal, conceptual formulations are useless. Buddhism has an immense repertoire of verbal, conceptual modes of pointing to the contents of Special Insight, all of which delight me because of their profundity and the way they point to what really does matter, what really is real. Initially, the Buddhist view illumined my suffering, an experience that is not an unusual route into Buddhist practice. Along the way, it provided a great deal of insight into how to think about gender issues effectively. Now it provides me with cogent ways to think about one of the pressing issues of our time, religious diversity.[7] In all cases, the words and concepts that can be so helpful arise out of experiences of utter stillness and equanimity that are so central to Buddhist sensibilities. This process – the insights that arise when one practises Buddhist disciplines and the way these insights illumine core issues of human existence – is, for me, the enduring delight of being a Buddhist.

That enduring delight, however, comes from something quite different from the sheer intellectual agility that dominates many academic contexts. Verbalizations of Special Insight are not quite the same as debating points. Their purpose is not to solve intellectual puzzles in which one is not personally invested. Rather, they are the tradition's best distillation of the experiences of its best minds – to be contemplated and investigated thoroughly, until one knows for sure, for oneself, whether they ring true or not. The process of contemplating and the encouragement to investigate for oneself mean that Buddhism is alive and that its insights can be applied to any situation or problem one might encounter. Thus, as I intimated earlier, I find Buddhist teachings too profound for me to be deterred by Buddhism's historical male dominance. And, in the long run, it has always been the Buddhist view that compels me to continue the journey, whatever other frustrations, especially reluctance even to acknowledge that Buddhism has gender issues, may continue to accompany me on my path.

In authentic Buddhism, that profound view and the accompanying practices are transmitted by a teacher. Nowadays, most or all of these teachings and practices are also available in books, but without personal instruction from a teacher it is difficult to grasp these teachings at a deep level. Anyone in the teaching profession should understand this immediately; individual attention and oral instruction are often critical if a student is to comprehend the material. Like many other wisdom traditions, Buddhism doubts the ability of written materials, by themselves, to convey deep insights and does not give final authority to texts. They are too easily perverted by the self-interest of the naive reader, as any consideration of the religious fundamentalisms common today in religions that give ultimate authority to a text should quickly indicate. Relying on their texts, religious leaders claim to have direct access to the mind of God and seek to dominate all people on the basis of their conviction that they have the truth for everyone. Buddhist teachers do not operate in this manner.

Buddhist teachers, including myself, often say that Buddhist teachings are extremely simply and basic – so simple that they are easily missed. Thus, it is as difficult to overestimate the importance of teachers in Buddhism as it is to overestimate the importance of personal verification of the relevance of what one has been taught. Though Buddhists regard teachers very highly, the purpose of a teacher is to help one discover what one is unlikely to discover on one's own, not to provide beliefs or ideologies for the student. (Buddhism is not a credal religion turning on correct beliefs in any case.) Without personal verification through examining one's own experiences, any profound teachings remain fundamentally irrelevant to the student. Thus, in Buddhism, as in many religious traditions that emphasize personal transformation through spiritual practices, the teacher–student relationship is subtle and profound. It is up to the student to discern that the teacher is trustworthy, not a spiritual fraud, and then to practise assigned disciplines seriously; the teacher has the responsibility to discern the student's needs accurately and not to be gratifying her or his own ego needs through having disciples.

In my work as a Buddhist feminist, I have always emphasized the importance of women teachers, for many reasons.[8] I have argued many times in the
past and I would still argue today that the most serious indicator of male
dominance in Buddhism historically has been the relative absence of female
teachers. I would also argue, as strongly as possible, that the bottom line
determining whether or not Buddhism has overcome its patriarchal tendencies is the presence of female teachers. It has been argued that because the
dharma is beyond gender, it doesn't matter whether women or men are the
teachers of that timeless, genderless dharma; the message would be the same
in any case. But I would argue that because the dharma is beyond gender,
therefore, one should expect that there would be about equal numbers
of women and men dharma teachers unless humanly constructed social
barriers are placed in the paths of women (or men). No other manifestation
of the claim that dharma is beyond gender makes sense. Why would there
be more men than women teachers of the timeless dharma that is beyond
gender? Yet throughout Buddhist history, women dharma teachers have
been relatively rare, though in contemporary North American Buddhism
about half the teachers of Buddhism are women.

In my own life as a Buddhist practitioner, I have worked with both female
and male teachers, though early in my practice life, my primary teacher
was a man whose activities were problematic to many women, Chogyam
Trungpa, Rinpoche. My own position has always been that, while theoreti-
cally, I would like to work with a woman teacher, ideology does not deter-
mine my choice of teachers. I would always become a student of the teacher
with whom I felt the closest relationship, the teacher who I felt offered the
clearest and most profound instruction in dharma, rather than seeking out a
woman teacher simply because she was a woman. In Buddhism, it is the
student's responsibility to choose a teacher carefully, so that one can then
trust the teacher. Ideology, even feminist ideology, is a poor guide to finding
someone worthy of trust.

Nevertheless, I was curious about the few women who did teach in the
Tibetan tradition and made an extra effort to meet them. Contrary to ideology, but consistent with good sense about dharma, I did not initially feel
especially compelled by these women *as* teachers. This pattern persisted
even when I met the woman who is now my principal teacher, and for whom
I now function as a senior teacher, Khandro Rinpoche. Now the relationship
fits the classic description of the teacher–student relationship in Tibetan
Buddhism and I am very happy about this development, which really did not
occur with either of my primary male teachers, despite years of serious study

and practice. But, despite my feminist viewpoint that the presence or absence of women teachers determines whether Buddhism is overcoming its heritage of male dominance, I am not convinced that my relationship with Khandro Rinpoche developed *because* she is a woman, but because she *is* the teacher that she is, as well as because of an apparent karmic link between us. That is as it should be.

I went to considerable effort to meet Khandro Rinpoche, because, like the dharma itself, she was not going to come to Eau Claire, Wisconsin. Another of many trips to Boulder, Colorado took me to meet her, and I was excited about the person I met, as well as about the fact that she strongly encouraged me to continue my work as a Buddhist feminist and promised she would help me with my practice. From that point on, I regarded her as one of my teachers, though my primary loyalties were with the Shambhala Buddhist organization in which I had grown up. She assumed the same thing about my primary identification and I actually became much more involved in the Shambhala organization while I also began to study seriously with Khandro Rinpoche, doing a major retreat with her every year. I was somewhat surprised, given my views about the importance of women teachers, that I continued to feel strongly connected with my male teachers even after I had found an ideal female teacher, but honesty is more important than ideology in Buddhist practice.

Then, eventually, many things converged and, somewhat against my earlier expectations, I began to realize how much I had learned from Khandro Rinpoche, how much major issues had been transmuted, and how much I was really in her world. At that point I began to consider her my primary teacher, though my other teachers also remain important. I think that this whole process is highly instructive regarding the actual relationship between ideology and authentic experience. It was good for me to learn that, whatever my belief system might be, I could regard a male teacher as my primary teacher even when a female teacher was also present. It is also good to know that when I came to regard Khandro Rinpoche as my primary teacher, it was because of her being the teacher she is, not because she is a woman. I am also delighted finally to have the kind of relationship with an authentic teacher for which I had always longed.

In sum, what is it about being a Buddhist that delights me so much? The profundity of its view, the transformative power of its spiritual disciplines, and the results – real change, a transformation from unhappiness to contentment. On the one hand, Buddhist disciplines bring taming of ideology and anger; and on the other hand, they bring a deepening of non-fixated passion for liberation – at all levels. Who could ask for more?

Notes

1. Over the years, I have found it critical to define what I mean by feminism, given the preconceptions and stereotypes about it that prevail, especially now in these times of backlash. I have used two general definitions for many years. First, feminism is about freedom from the prison of gender roles, from the notion that women automatically want certain things and behave in a certain way, while men automatically behave in a different way and want different things. Second, feminism is about the radical practice of the co-humanity of women and men. This means that all human options must be available to both women and men, without regard for cultural gender roles and expectations. This definition of feminism liberates men at least as much as it liberates women.

2. To formally become a Buddhist, one must take Refuge Vows in the presence of a preceptor and a witnessing *sangha* (community). The Three Jewels are *Buddha*, the example, *Dharma*, the reliable teachings, and *Sangha*, the community of companions.

3. The topic of 'karma' is easily misunderstood. Basically, it is about cause and effect, not only in the physical realm, but also in the moral realm. Karma is more about the negative effects of misconduct on the doer of those deeds than about the sufferings of unfortunate people, as is so often supposed. In the way that I have used the term in the above sentence, it means that for some reason, unexplainable by the theories of western science and social science, I have an incredibly strong affinity with some lineages of Tibetan Buddhism (and not with others). The traditional Buddhist explanation for such otherwise inexplicable affinities would invoke karma, the effects of relationships made in past lives.

4. This statement was made to me in the fall of 1968 by one of the professors of the history of religions at the University of Chicago, which was then the premier programme in comparative religions in the world.

5. Rita M. Gross, 1993, *Buddhism after Patriarchy: A Feminist History, Analysis, and Reconstruction*, Albany, NY: State University of New York Press, the first book-length discussion of women and Buddhism, is one of the most influential books on Buddhism and gender. It has affected both academic Buddhist studies and the practice of Buddhism.

6. This process is described in Rita M. Gross, 2000, 'The Female Body and Precious Human Birth: An Essay on Anger and Meditation', in Rita M. Gross, 2000, *Soaring and Settling: Buddhist Perspectives on Contemporary Social and Religious Issues*, New York: Continuum, pp. 7–12.

7. For example, see Rita M. Gross, 2005, 'Excuse Me, But What's the Question: Isn't Religious Diversity Normal?', in Paul Knitter (ed.), 2005, *The Myth of Religious Superiority: A Multifaith Exploration*, Maryknoll, NY: Orbis Books, pp. 75–87.

8. See *Buddhism after Patriarchy*, pp. 252–5.

VI. Women in World Religions: a Bibliography

Compiled by MARIE-THERES WACKER, with FRANZISKA BIRKE,
HEIKE HARBECKE AND JESSE PERILLO

Since 1980 the Catholic Theological Faculty of the University of Münster
has housed a library of works on the situation of women in world religions.
This was built up by Iris Müller, initially with only very modest financial
support. Since 1999, Marie-Theres Wacker (Theological Women's Studies)
and Annette Wilke (Religious Studies) have been looking after this library
and developed it. In addition, Münster has its own library of 'Christian
Feminist Theology'.

This bibliography (of books only, no journal articles) has been compiled
on the basis of the holdings of these two libraries. They are primarily of
books in German and English. This probably also reflects the fact that the
majority of academic titles are published in these two languages. Books in
other *Concilium*-languages have been included, in so far as we were aware of
them. In this area the bibliography needs further work.

The choice of subjects does not on the whole include books published
prior to 1995. Under the heading 'classics', however, we list some older titles
which have been foundational and groundbreaking. We have left out purely
historical studies and the area of goddess literature.

1. General titles

1.1 Journals

Journal of Feminist Studies in Religion (JFSR), Bloomington 1/1 (1985) ff.
Journal of Women and Religion, Berkeley 1/1 (1981) ff.
The Annual Review of Women in World Religions, Albany 1 (1991) – 6 (2002).

1.2 Classics

Nancy Auer Falk and Rita M. Gross (eds), 1980, *Unspoken Worlds: Women's
Religious Lives in Nonwestern Cultures*, San Francisco.

Ursula King (ed.), 1987, *Women in the World's Religions, Past and Present*, New York.

Arvind Sharma (ed.), 1987, *Women in World Religions*, McGill Studies in the History of Religions, Albany.

Arvind Sharma (ed.), 1994, *Today's Woman in World Religions*, McGill Studies in the History of Religions, Albany.

Arvind Sharma (ed.), 1994, *Religion and Women*, McGill Studies in the History of Religions, Albany.

1.3 Thematic monographs and edited volumes

Pamela Sue Anderson, 1998, *A Feminist Philosophy of Religion: The Rationality and Myths of Religious Belief*, Oxford.

Ulrike Bechmann, Sevda Demir and Gisela Egler, 2001, *Frauenkulturen: Christliche und muslimische Frauen in Begegnung und Gespräch*, Düsseldorf.

Brenda E. Brasher, 1998, *Godly Women: Fundamentalism and Female Power*, New Brunswick.

Judy Brink and Joan Mencher (eds), 1997, *Mixed Blessings: Gender and Religious Fundamentalism Cross Culturally*, New York.

Edith Castel, 1996, *L'éternité au feminine: La femme dans les religions*, Croire aujourd'hui Supplément 18, Paris.

Frances Devlin-Glass and Lyn McCredden (eds), 2001, *Feminist Poetics of the Sacred: Creative Suspicions*, Oxford.

Laura E. Donaldson, 2002, *Postcolonialism, Feminism, and Religious Discourse*, New York.

Shanin Gerami, 1996, *Women and Fundamentalism: Islam and Christianity*, New York.

Rita M. Gross and Rosemary Radford Ruether, 2001, *Religious Feminism and the Future of the Planet: A Christian–Buddhist Conversation*, London.

Yvonne Yazbeck Haddad, 2001, *Daughters of Abraham: Feminist Thought in Judaism, Christianity, and Islam*, Gainesville.

Jean Holm with John Bowker (eds), 1998, *Women in Religion*, Themes in Religious Studies, London.

Ursula King (ed.), 1995, *Religion and Gender*, Oxford.

Ulrike Krasberg, 1999, *Religion und weibliche Identität: Interdisziplinäre Perspektiven auf Wirklichkeiten*, Marburg.

Mehrézia Labidi-Maïza and Laurent Klein, 2004, *Abraham, réveille-toi, ils sont devenus fous!* Paris.

Sung-Hee Lee-Linke (ed.), 1999, *Ein Hauch der Kraft Gottes: Weibliche Weisheit in den Weltreligionen*, Frankfurt a.M.

Sung-Hee Lee-Linke, 1997, *Fenster zum Göttlichen: Weibliche Spiritualität in den Weltreligionen*, Neukirchen-Vluyn.

Ingrid Lukatis et al. (eds), 2000, *Religion und Geschlechterverhältnis*, Opladen.

Iris Müller and Ida Raming, 1998, *Aufbruch aus männlichen "Gottesordnungen":* *Reformbestrebungen von Frauen in christlichen Kirchen und im Islam*, Weinheim.

Oyèrónké Oyewumi, 1997, *The Invention of Women: Making an African Sense of Western Gender Discourses*, Minneapolis.

Irmgard Pahl (ed.), 2001, *Soziale Rollen von Frauen in Religionsgemeinschaften*, Münster.

Aloysius Pieris, 1996, *Feuer und Wasser: Frau, Gesellschaft, Spiritualität in Buddhismus und Christentum*, Theologie der dritten Welt 19, Freiburg.

Ataullah Siddiqui, 1998, *Christian–Muslim Dialogue in the Twentieth Century*, Basingstoke.

1.4 Post-Christian / Post-Jewish positions

Carol P. Christ, 2003, *She Who Changes: Reimagining the Divine in the World*, New York.

Mary Daly, 1978, *Gyn Ecology: The Metaethics of Radical Feminism*, Boston. Reissued with a new introduction: 1991, London.

Mary Daly, 1984, *Pure Lust: Elemental Feminist Philosophy*, Boston.

Mary Daly, 1994, *Outercourse: The Be-Dazzling Voyage*, San Francisco.

Daphne Hampson, 1996, *After Christianity*, London.

Starhawk (Miriam Simos), 1990, *Truth or Dare: Encounters with Power, Authority, and Mystery*, San Francisco.

2. Judaism

2.1 Journal

Lilith: The Jewish Women's Magazine, New York 1/1 (1976) ff.

2.2 Classics

Jutta Dick and Marina Sassenberg (eds), 1993, *Jüdische Frauen im 19. und 20. Jahrhundert: Lexikon zu Leben und Werk*, Reinbek bei Hamburg.

Blu Greenberg, 1983, *On Women and Judaism: A View from Tradition*, Philadelphia.

Susannah Heschel, 1983, *On Being a Jewish Feminist: A Reader*, New York.

Elizabeth Koltun (ed.), 1976, *The Jewish Woman: New Perspectives*, New York.

Pnina Navè Levinson, 1989, *Was wurde aus Saras Töchtern? Frauen im Judentum*, Gütersloh.

Pnina Navè Levinson, 1993, *Esther erhebt ihre Stimme: Jüdische Frauen beten*, Gütersloh.

Pnina Navè Levinson, 1992, *Eva und ihre Schwestern: Perspektiven einer jüdisch-feministischen Theologie*, Gütersloh.

Sally Priesand, 1975, *Judaism and the New Woman*, New York.

Judith Plaskow, 1990, *Standing Again at Sinai: Judaism from a Feminist Perspective*, San Francisco.

2.3 Series

A Feminist Companion to the Hebrew Bible, ed. Anthalya Brenner, Ser. 1, Sheffield 1993ff.; Ser. 2, Sheffield, 1998ff.
A Feminist Companion to the New Testament, ed. Amy Jill Levine, with Marianne Bickenstaff, Sheffield, 2001ff.

2.4 Thematic monographs and edited volumes

Penina V. Adelmann, 2nd edn 1996, *Miriam's Well: Rituals for Jewish Women around the Year*, New York.
Rachel Adler, 1999, *Engendering Judaism: An Inclusive Theology and Ethics*, Boston.
Marjorie Agosín, 1999, *Uncertain Travellers: Conversations with Jewish Women Immigrants to America*, Hanover, NH/London.
Rebecca T. Alpert, 1997, *Like Bread on the Seder Plate: Jewish Lesbians and the Transformation of Tradition*, New York.
Ariette Berdugo, 2002, *Juives et juifs dans le Maroc contemporain*, Paris.
Pauline Bébé (ed.), 2003, *Isha: Dictionnaire des femmes et du judaïsme*, Paris.
Sally Berkovic, 1997, *Straight Talk: My Dilemma as an Orthodox Jewish Woman*, Hoboken.
Susan Berrin, 1996, *Celebrating the New Moon: A Rosh Chodesh Anthology*, Northvale.
Rachel Biale, 1995, *Women and Jewish Law: The Essential Texts, Their History and Their Relevance for Today*, New York.
Leslie Brody, 1997, *Daughters of Kings: Growing up as a Jewish Woman in America*, Boston.
Esther M. Broner, 1999, *Bringing Home the Light: A Jewish Woman's Handbook of Rituals*, San Francisco.
Tamar Frankiel, 1995, *The Voice of Sarah: Feminine Spirituality and Traditional Judaism*, New York.
Esther Fuchs, 1999, *Women and the Holocaust: Narrative and Representation*, Studies in the Shoah 22, Lanham.
Marianne Goch, 2000, *Im Aufbruch: Biographien deutscher Jüdinnen*, Frankfurt a.M.
Karla Goldman, 2000, *Beyond the Synagogue Gallery: Finding a Place for Women in American Judaism*, Cambridge, MA.
Elyse Goldstein, 1998, *Revisions: Seeing Torah through a Feminist Lens*, Woodstock.
Elyse Goldstein, 2000, *The Women's Torah Commentary: New Insights from Women Rabbis on the 54 Weekly Torah Portions*, Woodstock.

Lynn Gottlieb, 1996, *She Who Dwells Within: A Feminist Vision of a Renewed Judaism*, New York.

Micah D. Halpern, 1998, *Jewish Legal Writings by Women*, Jerusalem.

Regina Jonas (Elisa Klapheck, ed.), 2000, *Fräulein Rabbiner Jonas: Kann die Frau das rabbinische Amt bekleiden? Eine Streitschrift*, Teetz.

Elisa Klapheck, 2005, *So bin ich Rabbinerin geworden: Jüdische Herausforderungen hier und jetzt*, Freiburg.

Lori Krafte-Jacobs, 1996, *Feminism and Modern Jewish Theological Method*, New York.

Laura Levitt, 1997, *Jews and Feminism: The Ambivalent Search for Home*, New York.

Silke Mertins, 1998, *Zwischentöne: Jüdische Frauenstimmen aus Israel*, Frankfurt a.M.

Miriam Peskowitz, 1997, *Judaism since Gender*, New York.

Miriam Peskowitz, 1997, *Spinning Fantasies: Rabbis, Gender, and History*, Berkeley, CA.

Melissa Raphael, 2003, *The Female Face of God in Auschwitz: A Jewish Feminist Theology of the Holocaust*, London and New York.

Hanna Rheinz, 1998, *Die jüdische Frau: Auf der Suche nach einer modernen Identität*, Gütersloh.

Faye Schulman, 1998, *Die Schreie meines Volkes in mir: Wie ich als jüdische Partisanin den Holocaust überlebte*, München.

Susan Starr Sered, 1996, *Women as Ritual Experts: The Religious Lives of Elderly Jewish Women in Jerusalem*, New York.

Sybil Sheridan, 1998, *Hear Our Voice: Women in the British Rabbinate*, Columbia and London.

Rachel Josefowitz Siegel (ed.), 1997, *Celebrating the Lives of Jewish Women: Patterns in a Feminist Sampler*, Haworth Innovations in Feminist Studies, New York.

Ingrid Strobl, 1998, *Die Angst kam erst danach: Jüdische Frauen im Widerstand in Europa 1939–1945*, Frankfurt a.M.

Sarah Silberstein Swartz (ed.), 1998, *From Memory to Transformation: Jewish Women's Voices*, Toronto.

Marianne Wallach-Faller, Doris Brodbeck and Yvonne Domhardt (eds), 2000, *Die Frau im Tallit: Judentum feministisch gelesen*, Zurich.

Rahel R. Wasserfall (ed.), 1999, *Women and Water: Menstruation in Jewish Life and Law*, Hanover, NH and London.

Gary Phillip Zola (ed.), 1996, *Women Rabbis: Exploration and Celebration: Papers Delivered at an Academic Conference Honoring Twenty Years of Women in the Rabbinate, 1972–1992*, Cincinatti.

3. Christianity

3.1 Selected journals

Der Apfel, Innsbruck 1/1 (1986) ff.
Ewha Journal of Feminist Theology (EJFT), Seoul 1/1 (1996) ff.
Fama: Feministisch-theologische Zeitschrift, Basel 1. (1985) ff.
Feminist Theology: The Journal of the Britain and Ireland School of Feminist Theology, Sheffield 1/1 (1992/93) ff.
In God's Image: Journal of Asian Women's Resource Centre for Culture and Theology, Seoul 1/1 (1982) ff.
Lectio difficilior: European Electronic Journal for Feminist Exegesis / Revue européenne électronique d'exégèse féministe / Europäische elektronische Zeitschrift für feministische Exegese, ed. Silvia Schroer, Bern 1 (2000) ff.
Mara: Tijdschrift voor feminisme en theologie, Kampen 1/1 (1987/88) ff.
Parvis: Chrétiens en liberté pour d'autres visages d'église, Paris 1/1 (1999) ff. (until 1999: *Femmes et hommes dans l'eglise*).
Schlangenbrut: Zeitschrift für feministisch und religiös interessierte Frauen (until 1/2002: *Streitschrift für feministisch und religiös interessierte Frauen*), Münster 1/1 (1983) ff.
Women-Church: An Australian Journal of Feminist Studies in Religion, Sydney 1/1 (1987) ff.
Yearbook / Journal of the European Society of Women in Theological Research / Jahrbuch der Europäischen Gesellschaft für die Theologische Forschung von Frauen / Annuaire de l'Association Européenne des femmes pour la recherché théologique, Kampen/ Mainz 1 (1993) ff; Leuven 6 (1998) ff.

3.2 Dictionaries

Elisabeth Gössmann, 2nd edn 2002, *Wörterbuch der feministischen Theologie*, Gütersloh.
Lisa Isherwood and Dorothea Mc Ewan (eds), 1996, *An A to Z of Feminist Theology*, Sheffield.
Letty M. Russell (ed.), 1996, *Dictionary of Feminist Theologies*, Louisville.

3.3 Selected series

Theologische Frauenforschung in Europa, ed. Hedwig Meyer-Wilmes and Marie-Theres Wacker, Münster, 2000ff.
Introductions in Feminist Theology, ed. Mary Grey, Lisa Isherwood, Catherine Norris and JanetWootton, Sheffield, 1995ff.

3.4 *Selected classics*

María Pilar Aquino (ed.), 1986, *Aportes para una teología desde la mujer: Conferencia Intercontinental de Mujeres Teólogas del Tercer Mundo*, Oaxtepec (México).

María Pilar Aquino, 1993, *Our Cry for Life: Feminist Theology from Latin* America, Maryknoll, NY.

Rita Nakashima Brock, 1994, *Journeys by Heart: A Christology of Erotic Power*, New York.

Katie G. Cannon, 1988, *Black Womanist Ethics*, Atlanta.

Hyun-Kyung Chung, 1991, *Struggle to Be the Sun Again: Introducing Asian Women's Theology*, London.

Mary Daly, 1968, *The Church and the Second Sex*, New York. With 'Feminist Postchristian Introduction' and 'New Archaic Afterwords', Boston, 1992.

Mary Daly, 1974, *Beyond God the Father: Toward a Philosophy of Women's Liberation*, Boston.

Virginia Fabella and Mercy Amba Oduyoye (eds), 1988, *With Passion and Compassion: Third World Women Doing Theology*, Maryknoll, NY.

Elisabeth Schüssler Fiorenza, 1983, revised new edn. 1992, *In Memory of Her: A Feminist Theological Reconstruction of Christian Origins*, London.

Ivoni Gebara, 1991, *As incomodas filhas de Eva na Igreja latinoamericana*, São Paolo.

Mary Grey, 1989, *Redeeming the Dream: Feminism, Redemption and Christian Tradition*, London.

Catharina Halkes, 1980, *Gott hat nicht nur starke Söhne: Grundzüge einer feministischen Theologie*, Gütersloh.

Carter Heyward, 1982, *The Redemption of God: A Theology of Mutual Relation*, Lanham.

Ada María Isasi-Díaz, 1993, *En la lucha: Elaborating a Mujerista theology: A Hispanic Women's Liberation Theology*, Minneapolis.

Ursula King (ed.), 1994, *Feminist Theology from the Third World: A Reader*, London.

Elisabeth Moltmann-Wendel, 1978, *Menschenrechte für die Frau*, Munich.

Mercy Amba Oduyoye and Musimbi Kanyoro (eds), 1990, *Talitha, Qumi! Proceedings of the Convocation of African Women Theologians 1989*, Ibadan.

Rosemary Radford Ruether, 1974, *Religion and Sexism: Images of Woman in the Jewish and Christian Tradition*, New York.

Rosemary Radford Ruether, 1983, *Sexism and God-Talk: Toward a Feminist Theology*, London 1983.

Helen Schüngel-Straumann, 1989, *Die Frau am Anfang: Eva und die Folgen*, Freiburg.

Delores S. Williams, 1993, *Sisters in the Wilderness: The Challenge of Womanist God Talk*, Maryknoll.

3.5 Thematic monographs and edited volumes

Marcella Althaus-Reid, 2004, *From Feminist Theology to Indecent Theology: Readings on Poverty, Sexual Identity and God*, London.

Marcella Althaus-Reid, 2003, *The Queer God*, London.

Regina Ammicht-Quinn, 2nd edn 2001, *Körper, Religion, Sexualität: Theologische Reflexionen zur Ethik der Geschlechter*, Mainz.

Esperanza Bautista, 1999, *El ecumenismo y la teología feminista*, Bilbao.

Elizabeth Behr-Sigel and Kallistos Ware, 2000, *The Ordination of Women in the Orthodox Church*, Geneva.

Kari Elisabeth Børresen (ed.), 1995, *The Image of God: Gender Models in Judaeo-Christian Tradition*, Minneapolis.

Sabine Demel, 2004, *Frauen und kirchliches Amt: Vom Ende eines Tabus in der katholischen Kirche*, Freiburg.

Musa W. Dube, 2001, *Other Ways of Reading: African Women and the Bible*, Atlanta.

Musa W. Dube, 2000, *Postcolonial Feminist Interpretation of the Bible*, St Louis.

Nancy L. Eiesland, 1998, *The Disabled God: Toward a Liberatory Theology of Disability*, Nashville.

Ivone Gebara, 1999, *Le mal au féminin: Réflexions théologiques à partir du féminisme*, Paris.

Elisabeth Gössmann (ed.), 1984ff, *Archiv für philosophie- und theologiegeschichtliche Frauenforschung*, Munich.

Jacquelyn Grant, 1995, *Perspectives on Womanist Theology*, Atlanta.

Mary Grey, 2001, *Introducing Feminist Images of God*, Sheffield.

Andrea Günter, Ina Praetorius and Ulrike Wagener (eds), 1998, *Weiberwirtschaft weiterdenken: Feministische Ökonomiekritik als Arbeit am Symbolischen*, Luzern.

Carter Heyward, 1996, *Speaking of Christ: A Lesbian Feminist Voice*, Cleveland.

Lisa Isherwood and Elizabeth Stuart, 1998, *Introducing Body Theology*, Sheffield.

Elizabeth A. Johnson, 1994, *She Who Is: The Mystery of God in Feminist Theological Discourse*, New York.

Elizabeth A. Johnson, 1998, *Friends of God and Prophets: A Feminist Theological Reading of the Communion of Saints*, New York and London.

Elizabeth A. Johnson, 2004, *Truly Our Sister: A Theology of Mary in the Communion of Saints*, New York.

Musimbi R. A. Kanyoro, 2002, *Introducing Feminist Cultural Hermeneutics: An African Perspective*, Sheffield.

Christina Kayales, 1998, *Gottesbilder von Frauen auf den Philippinen: Die Bedeutung der Subjektivität für eine interkulturelle Hermeneutik*, Münster.

Kwok Pui-lan, 1995, *Discovering the Bible in the Non-Biblical World*, Maryknoll, NY.

Kwok Pui-lan, 2005, *Postcolonial Imagination and Feminist Theology*, Louisville.

Élisabeth J. Lacelle and Nicole Bourbonnais (eds), 1983, *La femme, son corps, la religion: Approches pluridisciplinaires*, Montréal.

Irene Leicht, Claudia Rakel and Stefanie Rieger-Goertz (eds), 2003, *Arbeitsbuch feministische Theologie: Inhalte, Methoden und Materialien für Hochschule, Erwachsenenbildung und Gemeinde*, Gütersloh.

Teresa Martinho Toldy, 1998, *Deus e a palavra de Deus na teologia feminista*, Lisboa.

Carol Meyers and Sharon Ringe (eds), 2nd edn 1998, *The Women's Bible Commentary*, London/Louisville.

Hedwig Meyer-Wilmes, 1996, *Zwischen lila und lavendel: Schritte feministischer Theologie*, Ratisbonne.

Cettina Militello (ed.), 2004, *Donna e teologia: bilancio di un secolo*, Bologna.

Mercedes Navarro Puerto and Pilar de Miguel (eds), 2004, *10 palabras clave en teología feminista*, Estella (Navarra).

Mercy Amba Oduyoye, 2001, *Introducing African Women's Theology*, Sheffield.

Haruko Okano, 2002, *Christliche Theologie im japanischen Kontext*, Frankfurt and London.

Ofelia Ortega, 1995, *Women's Visions: Theological Reflection, Celebration, Action*, Geneva.

Anne-Marie Pelletier, 2001, *Le Christianisme et les femmes: vingt siècles d'histoire*, Paris.

Ina Praetorius, 2005, *Handeln aus der Fülle: Postpatriarchale Ethik in biblischer Tradition*, Gütersloh.

Rosemary Radford Ruether, 1998, *Women and Redemption: A Theological History*, Minneapolis.

Rosemary Radford Ruether, 1998, *Introducing Redemption in Christian Feminism*, Sheffield.

Dorothea Reininger, 1999, *Diakonat der Frau in der einen Kirche: Diskussionen, Entscheidungen und pastoral-praktische Erfahrungen in der christlichen Ökumene und ihr Beitrag zur römisch-katholischen Diskussion*, Ostfildern.

José Ignacio Saranyana, 2000, *Teología de la mujer, teología feminista, teología mujerista y ecofeminismo en América latina (1975 - 2000)*, San José.

Luise Schottroff and Marie-Theres Wacker (eds), 2nd edn 1998, *Kompendium feministische Bibelauslegung*, Gütersloh. (American edition in preparation with Eerdmans.)

Luise Schottroff, 1995, *Lydia's Impatient Sisters: A Feminist Social History of Early Christianity*, Louisville.

Silvia Schroer, Silvia and Sophia Bietenhard (eds), 2003, *Feminist Interpretation of the Bible and the Hermeneutics of Liberation*, JSOTS 374, Sheffield.

Elisabeth Schüssler Fiorenza (ed.), 1993 and 1994, *Searching the Scriptures*, New York and London.

Elisabeth Schüssler Fiorenza, 2001, *Wisdom Ways: Introducing Feminist Biblical Interpretation*, Maryknoll.

Elsa Tamez, 1991, *Contra toda condena: la justificación por la fe desde los excluidos*, San José.

Elsa Tamez, 1998, *Cuando los horizontes se cierran: Eclesiastes o qohelet*, San José.

Ana Maria Tepedino (ed.), 1998, *Entre la indignación y la esperanza. Teología Feminista Latinoamericana*, Santafé de Bogotá.

Elina Vuola, 2001, *Limits of Liberation: Praxis as Method in Latin American Liberation Theology and Feminist Theology*, London.

Eske Wollrad, 2005, *Weißsein im Widerspruch: Feministische Perspektiven auf Rassismus, Kultur und Religion*, Königstein im Taunus.

4. Islam

4.1 Encyclopaedia

Suad Joseph (ed.), 2003–2006, *Encyclopedia of Women & Islamic Cultures*, three vols, Leiden.

4.2 Selected classics

Nawal El Saadawi, 1997, *The Hidden Face of Eve: Women in the Arab World* (1st English edn 1980), Trowbridge.

Fatima Mernissi, rev. edn 1987, *Beyond The Veil: Male–Female Dynamics in Modern Muslim Society* (1975), South Bend.

Fatima Mernissi, 1993, *The Forgotten Queens of Islam*, University of Minnesota Press.

Annemarie Schimmel, 1997, *My Soul Is a Woman: The Feminine in Islam*, New York and London.

Margaret Smith 1928, *Rabi'a the Mystic and Her Fellow-Saints in Islam : Being the Life and Teachings of Rabi'a al-'Adawiyya Al Qaysiyya of Basra*, Cambridge; new edn Cambridge, 1984.

Wiebke Walther, 1980, 3rd rev. edn 1997, *Die Frau im Islam*, Leipzig.

4.3 Thematic monographs and edited volumes

Lise J. Abid, 2001, *Journalistinnen im Tschador: Frauen und gesellschaftlicher Aufbruch im Iran*, Frankfurt.

Farideh Akashe-Böhme, 2002, *Die islamische Frau ist anders: Vorurteile und Realitäten*, Gütersloh.

Alessandro Aruffo, 2000, *Donne e islam*, Rome.

Sharma Arvind (ed.), 2002, *Women in Indian Religions*, Oxford.

Amira el Azhary Sonbol (ed.), 1996, *Women, the Family, and Divorce Laws in Islamic History*, Syracuse, NY.

Leila Babès, 1997, *L'Islam positif: La religion des jeunes musulmans de France*, Paris.

Leila Babès, 2004, *Le voile démystifié*, Paris.

Asma Barlas, 2002, *"Believing Women" in Islam*, Austin.

Marion Baumgart, 1991, *Wie Frauen Frauen sehen: Westliche Forscherinnen bei arabischen Frauen*, Frankfurt a.M.

Cheryl Benard and Edit Schlaffer, 2002, *"Die Politik ist ein wildes Tier": Afghanische Frauen kämpfen um ihre Zukunft*, Munich.

Frauke Biehl, 1999, *Muslimische Frauen in Deutschland erzählen über ihren Glauben*, Gütersloh.

Khalil Darwish and Karlhans Liebl, 1991, *Die "neue" Verschleierung der arabischen Frau: Eine Untersuchung zu den Gründen für die Renaissance des "el-Hijab" in Jordanien*, Pfaffenweiler.

Christèle Dedebant, 2003, *Le voile et la bannière: L'avant-garde féministe au Pakistan*, Paris.

Nawal El Saadawi, 1997, *The Nawal El Saadawi Reader*, London and New York. (Enlarged German edn, 2002, *Fundamentalismus gegen Frauen: Die 'Löwin vom Nil' und ihr Kampf für die Menschenrechte der Frau*, Kreuzlingen and Munich.)

Elizabeth Warnock Fernea, 1998, *In Search of Islamic Feminism: One Woman's Global Journey*, New York.

Yvonne Yazbeck Haddad, 1998, *Islam, Gender, and Social Change*, New York.

Taj ul-Islam Hashmi, 2000, *Women and Islam in Bangladesh: Beyond Subjection and Tyranny*, Basingstoke.

Ayaan Hirsi Ali, 2004, *De maagdenkooi*, Amsterdam (German edn, 2005, *Ich klage an: Plädoyer für die Befreiung der muslimischen Frauen*, Munich).

Ayaan Hirsi Ali, 2004, *Submission: De tekst, de reacties en de achtergronden*, Amsterdam.

Gabriele Hofmann, 1997, *Muslimin werden: Frauen in Deutschland konvertieren zum Islam*, Frankfurt a.M.

Arthur Frederick Ide, 1996, *The Qur'an on Woman, Marriage, Birth Control and Divorce*, Women in History 24, Las Colinas.

Haifaa A. Jawad, 2001, *The Rights of Women in Islam: An Authentic Approach*, Basingstoke.

Zahra Kamalkhani, 1998, *Women's Islam: Religious Practice among Women in Today's Iran*, London.

Yasemin Karakaşoğlu-Aydın, 2000, *Muslimische Religiosität und Erziehungsvorstellungen: Eine empirische Untersuchung zu Orientierungen bei türkischen Lehramts- und Pädagogik-Studentinnen in Deutschland*, Frankfurt.

Ruth Klein-Hessling (ed.), 1999, *Der neue Islam der Frauen: Weibliche Lebenspraxis in der globalisierten Moderne; Fallstudien aus Afrika, Asien und Europa*, Bielefeld.

Gritt Maria Klinkhammer, 2000, *Moderne Formen islamischer Lebensführung: Eine qualitativ-empirische Untersuchung zur Religiosität sunnitisch geprägter Türkinnen der zweiten Generation in Deutschland*, Marburg.

Claudia Knieps, 1999, *Geschichte der Verschleierung der Frau im Islam*, Würzburg.

Eva Künzler, 1999, *Zum westlichen Frauenbild von Musliminnen*, Würzburg.

Sabine Küper-Basgöl, 1992, *Frauen in der Türkei zwischen Feminismus und Reislamisierung*, Münster.

B. Aisha Lemu and Fatima Grimm, 1996, *Frau und Familienleben im Islam*, Munich.

Samsam Renate Makowski and Stefan Makowski, 1996, *Sufismus für Frauen: Zugänge zur islamischen Mystik*, Zurich.

Christine Mallouhi, 1999, *Mode, Mütter und Muslime: Mit Muslimen leben*, Giessen.

Christiane Paulus, 1999, *Interreligiöse Praxis postmodern: Eine Untersuchung muslimisch–christlicher Ehen in der BRD*, Frankfurt a.M.

Editha Platte, 2000, *Frauen in Amt und Würden: Handlungsspielräume muslimischer Frauen im ländlichen Nordostnigeria*, Frankfurt a.M.

Peter Priskil, 1994, *Taslima Nasrin: Der Mordaufruf und seine Hintergründe*, Freiburg i. Br.

Barbara Pusch, 2001, *Die neue muslimische Frau: Standpunkte & Analysen*, Würzburg.

Hans-Peter Raddatz, 2005, *Allahs Frauen: Djihad zwischen Scharia und Demokratie*, Munich.

Ruth Roded, 1999, *Women in Islam and the Middle East: A Reader*, London.

Bettina Rühl, 1997, *Wir haben nur die Wahl zwischen Wahnsinn oder Widerstand: Frauen in Algerien*, Unkel (Rhein).

Nausikaa Schirilla, 1996, *Die Frau, das Andere der Vernunft? Frauenbilder in der arabisch-islamischen und europäischen Philosophie*, Frankfurt a.M.

Christine Schirrmacher and Ursula Spuler-Stegemann, 2004, *Frauen und die Scharia: Die Menschenrechte im Islam*, Munich.

Claudia Schöning-Kalender (ed.), 1997, *Feminismus, Islam, Nation: Frauenbewegungen im Maghreb, in Zentralasien und in der Türkei*, Frankfurt a.M.

Karimah Katja Stauch, 2004, *Die Entwicklung einer islamischen Kultur in Deutschland: Eine empirische Untersuchung anhand von Frauenfragen*, Berlin.

Holger Vagt, 1992, *Die Frau in Saudiarabien zwischen Tradition und Moderne*, Berlin.

Angelika Vauti and Lise J. Abid (eds), 1999, *Frauen in islamischen Welten: Eine Debatte zur Rolle der Frau in Gesellschaft, Politik und Religion*, Frankfurt a.M.

Amina Wadoud, 2006, *Inside the Gender Jihad: Women's Reform in Islam*, Oxford.

Amina Wadoud, 1996, *Qu'ran and Woman. Rereading the Sacred Text from a Woman's Perspective*, Oxford.

Stephanie Waletzki, 2001, *Ehe und Ehescheidung in Tunesien: Zur Stellung der Frau in Recht und Gesellschaft*, Berlin.

Karin Werner, 1997, *Between Westernization and the Veil: Contemporary Lifestyles of Women in Cairo*, Bielefeld.

Katja Werthmann, 1997, *Nachbarinnen: Die Alltagswelt muslimischer Frauen in einer nigerianischen Großstadt*, Frankfurt a.M.

5. Hinduism

5.1 Journal

Manushi: A Journal about Women and Society, Delhi 1/1 1979 ff.

5.2 Classics

Lynn Bennett, 1983, *Dangerous Wives and Sacred Sisters: Social and Symbolic Roles of Women in Nepal*, New York (*see also*: Grodzins Gold).
Narendra Nath Bhattacharyya, 1974, *History of the Sakta Religion*, New Delhi.
N. Shanta, 1997, *The Unknown Pilgrims: The Voice of the Sadhvis, the History, Spirituality and Life of the Jaina Women Ascetics*, Delhi.

5.3 Thematic monographs and edited volumes

Anant Sadashiv Altekar, 1995, *The Position of Women in Hindu Civilization: From Prehistoric Times to the Present Day*, Delhi.
Sharma Arvind (ed.), 2005, *Goddesses and Women in the Indic Religious Tradition*, Leiden.
Sharma Arvind (ed.), 2002, *Women in Indian Religions*, Oxford.
Carmel Berkson, 1997, *The Divine and Demoniac: Mahisa's Heroic Struggle with Durga*, Delhi.
Marine Carrin, 1997, *Enfants de la Déesse: dévotion et prêtrise féminines au Bengale*, Paris.
Maitrayee Chaudhuri (ed.), 2004, *Feminism in India*, Women Unlimited, New Delhi.
Eunice De Souza (ed.), 2004, *Purdah: An Anthology*, Delhi, New York and Oxford.
Lynn Teskey Denton, 2004, *Female Ascetics in Hinduism*, SUNY Series in Hindu Studies, Albany NY.
Ann Grodzins Gold and Gloria Goodwin Raheja, 1994, *Listen to the Heron's Words: Reimagining Gender and Kinship in North India*, Berkeley, CA.
Charus Smita Gupta, 2002, *Sexuality, Obscenity, Community: Women, Muslims, and the Hindu Public in Colonial India*, New York.
Birgit Heller, 1999, *Heilige Mutter und Gottesbraut: Frauenemanzipation im modernen Hinduismus*, Vienna.
Alf Hiltebeitel and Kathleen M. Erndl (eds), 2002, *Is the Goddess a Feminist? The Politics of South Asian Goddesses*, New Delhi.
Meena Khandelwl, 2004, *Women in Ochre Robes: Gendering Hindu Renunciation*, SUNY Series in Hindu Studies, Albany/NY.
David R. Kinsley, 1997, *Tantric Visions of the Divine Feminine: The Ten Mahāvidyās*, Berkeley, CA.
Branislava Laux, 1998, *Die Frau in der Hindugesellschaft zwischen Tradition und Moderne: Eine Untersuchung zu ihrer sozialen und politischen Stellung*, Munich.

Swami Madhavananda, 1997, *Great Women of India: The Holy Mother Birth Centenary Memorial*, Calcutta.

Svami Nikhilananda, 1997, *Holy Mother: Being the Life of Sri Sarada Devi, Wife of Sri Ramakrishna and Helpmate in His Mission*, New York.

Anne Mackenzie Pearson, 1996, *"Because It Gives Me Peace of Mind": Ritual Fasts in the Religious Lives of Hindu Women*, Albany..

Karen Pechilis (ed.), 2004, *The Graceful Guru: Hindu Female Gurus in India and the United States*, New York.

Katharina Poggendorf-Kakar, 2001, *Göttin, Gattin, Mutter: Hinduistische Frauen der urbanen Mittelschicht im sozio-religiösen Kontext*, Berlin.

Anupama Rao (ed.), 2005, *Gender and Caste*, London.

Madhavi Renavikar, 2003, *Women and Religion: A Sociological Analysis*, Jaipur.

Steven J. Rosen, 1999, *Vaisnavi: Women and the Worship of Krishna*, Delhi.

Swami Saradesananda and J. N. Dey, 2000, *The Mother, as I Saw Her (Being Reminiscences of the Holy Mother Sri Sarada Devi)*, Mylapore.

N. Shanta, 1997, *The Unknown Pilgrims: The Voice of the Sadhvis, the History, Spirituality and Life of the Jaina Women Ascetics*, Delhi.

Wendy Sinclair-Brull, 1997, *Female Ascetics: Hierarchy and Purity in an Indian Religious Movement*, Richmond.

6. Buddhism, Confucianism, Shinto

6.1 Classics

Rita M. Gross, 1993, *Buddhism after Patriarchy: A Feminist History, Analysis, and Reconstruction of Buddhism*, Albany.

Sung-Hee Lee-Linke, 1991, *Frauen gegen Konfuzius: Perspektiven einer asiatisch-feministischen Theologie*, Gütersloh.

Haruko K. Okano, 1976, *Die Stellung der Frau im Shinto: Eine religionsphänomenologische und -soziologische Untersuchung*, Studies in Oriental Religions 1, Wiesbaden.

6.2 Thematic monographs and edited volumes

Lee-Whan Ahn, 1997, *Von der tugendhaften zur gebildeten Frau: Kontinuität und Wandel in der Frauenbildung Koreas um die Wende vom 19. Jahrhundert zum 20. Jahrhundert – eine Untersuchung unter Frauenemanzipatorischem Aspekt*, Frankfurt a.M.

Ellison Banks Findly (ed.), 2000, *Women's Buddhism, Buddhism's Women: Traditions, Revision, Renewal*, Boston.

June Campbell, 1996, *Traveller in Space: In Search of Female Identity in Tibetan Buddhism*, London.

Marianne Dresser, 1996, *Buddhist Women on the Edge: Contemporary Perspectives from the Western Frontier*, Berkeley.

Lenore Friedman and Charlotte Joko Beck, 1997, *Being Bodies: Buddhist Women on the Paradox of Embodiment*, Boston.

André Golomb, 1998, *Buddha und die Frauen: Nonnen und Laienfrauen in den Darstellungen der Pali-Literatur*, Altenberge 1998.

Isaline B. Horner, 1999, *Women under Primitive Buddhism: Laywomen and Almswomen*, Delhi.

Manfred Hutter (ed.), 1998, *Die Rolle des Weiblichen in der indischen und buddhistischen Kulturgeschichte: Akten des Religionswissenschaftlichen Symposiums 'Frau und Göttin' in Graz (15.-16. Juni 1997)*, Graz.

Ayya Khema, 1998, *I Give You My Life: The Autobiography of a Western Buddhist Nun*, Boston.

Hae-Soon Kim, 2005, *Geschlechterbeziehungen in der traditionellen Gesellschaft Koreas zwischen schamanischem Weltbild und konfuzianischer Gesellschaftslehre*, Frankfurt.

Dorothy Ko (ed.), 2003, *Women and Confucian Cultures in Premodern China, Korea, and Japan*, Berkeley.

Karma Lekshe Tsomo (ed.), 2000, *Innovative Buddhist Women: Swimming against the Stream*, Curzon Critical Studies in Buddhism, Richmond, Surrey.

Karma Lekshe Tsomo, 1999, *Buddhist Women across Cultures: Realizations*, Albany.

Thea Mohr, 2002, *Weibliche Identität und Leerheit: Eine ideengeschichtliche Rekonstruktion der buddhistischen Frauenbewegung Sakyadhitā International*, Frankfurt, Brussels and Oxford.

Tscheng-Tsu Schang, 1996, *Chinas weise Frauen: Heilerin, Schamanin, Priesterin*, Berne.

Miranda Shaw, 1994, *Passionate Enlightment: Woman in Tantric Buddhism*, Princeton.

Masatoshi Ueki, 2001, *Gender Equality in Buddhism*, New York.

Joanne C. Watkins, 1996, *Spirited Women: Gender, Religion, and Cultural Identity in the Nepal Himalaya*, New York.

Liz Wilson, 1996, *Charming Cadavers: Horrific Figurations of the Feminine in Indian Buddhist Hagiographic Literature*, Chicago.

Contributors

VIRGINIA RAQUEL AZCUY was born in Argentina in 1961 and gained a doctorate in dogmatic theology from the Argentine Catholic University (UCA) in Buenos Aires in 1996. She has lectured on spiritual theology at UCA since 2003 and has held various teaching posts at other theological institutes. From 2002 to 2004 she researched for UCA's 'The Argentine Social Debt' programme. Since 2003 she has been general coordinator of the '*Teologanda*' programme of study, research and publication, and, from 2006, theological examiner at the Elizalde Higher Institute. Her publications include *La figura de Teresa de Lisieux: Ensayo de fenomenología teológica según H. U. Von Baltasar* (2 vols, 1997) and three volumes published by '*Teologanda*' as separate issues of *Proyecto* (39, 2001; 44, 2003; 45, 2004).

Address: Pontificia Universidad Cátolica Argentinia, Facùltad de Teologia, Concordia 4422 (C14 19 AOH), Ciudad de Buenos Aires, Argentina.
E-mail: vra@inforia.com.ar.

RITA M. GROSS is Professor Emerita of Religion and Philosophy at the University of Wisconsin-Eau Claire, a specialist in comparative religions, the author of *Buddhism After Patriarchy* (Albany 1993), *Soaring and Settling* (Continuum 1998) and *Religion, Feminism and the Future of the Planet* (with Rosemary Ruether, Continuum 2001). She holds a PhD from the University of Chicago and is a practitioner of Vajrayana Buddhism.

Address: 126 Gilbert Ave, Eau Claire, WI 54701, USA.
E-mail: rmg@ritamgross.com

LINA GUPTA is professor of Philosophy at Glendale College. She has taught at California State University, at Loyola Mary Mount University, at Hsi Lai University and at Claremont University. Born and educated in India, she graduated from the University of Calcutta, India with a major in philosophy and received her doctorate in Asian and Comparative Philosophy from Claremont University, Claremont, California. Her research focuses on Hinduism and feminism, in particular ecofeminism. Dr Gupta has published articles on various Hindu goddesses and Hindu rituals.

Address: Philosophy Department Chair, Professor of Philosophy, San Rafael 338 1500 North Urdigo Road, Glendale, CA 91208, USA.
Email: lgupta@glendale.edu

HILLE HAKER is Professor of Moral Theology/Social Ethics at the Catholic Faculty of Frankfurt, and a member of the European Group on Ethics in Sciences and New Technologies (EGE). From 2003 to 2005 she was Associate Professor of Christian Ethics, Harvard University, Cambridge, MA (USA). She studied Catholic theology, German literature and philosophy at the Universities of Tübingen, Munich and Nijmegen (NL). From 1989 to 2003 she was staff member of the Center for Ethics in the Sciences and Humanities, and lecturer at the Department of Ethics/Social Ethics at the Catholic Theological Faculty, both University of Tübingen. Her books include *Moralische Identität* (1999), *Ethik der genetischen Frühdiagnostik* (2002) and three co-edited volumes: *Ethics of Human Genome Analysis: European Perspectives* (1993), *The Ethics of Genetics in Human Procreation* (2000) and *Ethik-Geschlecht-Wissenschaften* (2006).

Address: Fachbereich Katholische Theologie – Lehrstuhl Ethik, Grüneburgplatz 1 - 60323 Frankfurt, Germany.
E-mail: h.haker@em.uni-frankfurt.de

KATERINA KARKALA-ZORBA was born in 1961 in Volos in Greece and grew up in Kehl/ Rhein in Germany. She obtained master's degrees in Français Langue Etrangère in Paris in 1988 and in Ecumenical Theology in Thessaloniki in 2003. She is now Director of Studies at the Academy in Volos with responsibility for conferences, theological seminars (Academy for Theological Studies) and adult education for women. She is preparing to study for a doctorate at the Theology Faculty in Thessaloniki together with the Orthodox Seminary at the University of Munich. She is a member of various committees of the Greek Orthodox Church on diocesan and national levels and of a number of ecumenical committees and organizations.

Address: Kassaveti 147, 38221 Volos, Greece.

MADHU KHANNA, who holds a doctorate from Oxford University, is Associate Professor at the Indira Gandhi National Centre for the Arts, New Delhi, and director of Narivada, the Gender, Culture and Civilization Network (IGNCA). Her areas of research include tantric symbolism and goddess ecology.

Address: Indira Gandhi National Centre for the Arts, Janpath, New Delhi, 10001, India.
E-mail: khanna_madhu@yahoo.com

YOUNG-MI KIM was born in 1957 in Cheonju, Korea. She graduated from the College of Liberal Arts of Ewha Woman's University, majoring in history, and achieved an MA and a doctorate from the same institution. She is currently Professor of History at Ewha. Her major works include *The History of Buddhism of Silla*, and she co-authored *Methodology of Korean Thought*, *Temple Seongju and Nanghye*. She writes mainly on the influence of Buddhism on Koryeo women, the Buddhist monks' outlook on women, and the practice of Buddhist nuns.

Address: Ewha Women's University, 11-1 Daehyun-Dong, Seodaemun-Ku, Seoul 120-750, South Korea.

ELISA KLAPHECK was born in 1962 in Düsseldorf and studied politics and Jewish studies. For several years she worked as a journalist for German daily newspapers such as the Berlin *Tagesspiegel* and the *taz*, later for television and radio. From 1998 she was the editor of the monthly magazine *jüdisches berlin*. In 1999, together with Lara Dämmig and Rachel Herweg, she organized 'Bet Debora Berlin', the first conference of European female rabbis, cantors and Jewish women who had either undertaken rabbinic studies or were interested in doing so. So far two further conferences have been organized (2000 and 2001). Her most recent publication is *So bin ich Rabbinerin geworden: Jüdische Herausforderungen hier und jetzt* (Freiburg: Herder, 2005). In January 2004 she was ordained as a rabbi in the USA. Since May 2005 she has been living in Amsterdam.

Address: Sandhorst 34, 1082 BL Amsterdam, The Netherlands.

MEHRÉZIA LABIDI-MAÏZA was born in Tunisia in 1963 and holds a diploma in English language and literature from the University of Tunis and in French language and literature from La Sorbonne Nouvelle in Paris. She is a trans-

lator specializing in technical, legal and religious texts, and engaged in inter-
faith dialogue in France. She has co-authored several books, including (with
Laurent Klein) *Abraham, réveille-toi, ils sont devenus fous!* (2004); (with
Claude Geffré) *Y a-t-il quelque chose après la mort?* (2004); (with Alain
Houziaux *et al.*) *La religion peut-elle render heureux?* (2003).

Address: 07, rue de Kabylie, F-75019 Paris, France.

HAMIDEH MOHAGHEGHI was born in 1954 in Teheran, Iran, where she later
studied law. She also studied law, religious studies and Islamic theology in
Hanover and Hamburg. She has lived in Germany since 1977 and is in
demand as a speaker on issues of interfaith dialogue, and is a Muslim representative on political and church committees such as the 'Arbeitskreis
Christen and Muslime' of the Zentralkommittee der Deutschen Katholiken.
She is also Vice-President of 'Huda', a network of Muslim women in
Germany, and has published on Islam in Germany and gender relationships
in Islam.

Address: Querstr. 18, 30519 Hannover, Germany.

ANNE J. NASIMIYU-WASIKE is a Kenyan and belongs to a Ugandan Religious
Institute of the Little Sisters of St Francis of Assisi. She has lectured at
Kenyatta University in the Department of Religious Studies since 1987. Her
areas of research are Theology of Inculturation and African Women's
Theology. She has served her Religious Institute as General Superior
(1992–98). She has also served Kenyatta University as Dean of Students
(1999–2003). She is a member of the Circle of Concerned African Women
Theologians and the Ecumenical Association of Third World Theologians.

Address: Mt Alverna Convent, PO Box 1520, Eldoret, Kenya.
E-mail: anasimiyu@yahoo.com

ADELE REINHARTZ is the Associate Vice-President for Research at the
University of Ottawa, where she also holds the position of Professor in the
Department of Classics and Religious Studies. Her main areas of research
are John's Gospel, early Jewish–Christian relations, feminist criticism, and,
most recently, the Bible and film. She is the author of numerous articles and
several books, including *'Why Ask My Name?' Anonymity and Identity in
Biblical Narrative* (Oxford University Press, 1998), *Befriending the Beloved
Disciple: A Jewish Reading of the Gospel of John* (Continuum, 2001) and

Scripture on the Silver Screen (Westminster John Knox, 2003). Her latest book is a study of the Jesus movies, entitled *Jesus of Hollywood*, which will be published by Oxford University Press in 2006. She is currently working on a book on Caiaphas the High Priest, in History, Historiography and Culture, with support from the Social Sciences and Humanities Research Council. Adele was elected to the Royal Society of Canada in 2005.

Address: Départment d'Etudes anciennes et de Sciences des religions, Tabaret Hall, Room 24613, University of Ottawa, 550 Cumberland, Ottawa, Ontario K1N6N5 Canada.
E-mail: Adele.Reinhartz@uottawa.ca

SUSAN ROSS is Professor of Theology at Loyola University Chicago and the author of *Extravagant Affections: A Feminist Sacramental Theology* (New York, 1998) and of numerous articles and book chapters on women, gender, embodiment and sacramentality.

Address: Loyola University of Chicago, 6525 N. Sheridan Road, Chicago, IL 60626, USA.
E-mail: sross@wpo.it.luc.edu

MARIE-THERES WACKER is professor for Old Testament and Theological Women's Studies at the Catholic Theological Faculty of the University of Münster, Germany. She is the author of numerous publications about the feminist interpretation of the Bible, Jewish–Christian dialogue and the debate about the monotheism of Israel.

Address: Katholisch-Theologische Fakultät, Seminar für Theologische Frauenforschung, Westfälische Wilhelms-Universität Münster, Hüfferstraße 27, 48149 Münster, Germany.
E-mail: femtheo@uni-muenster.de

Of the many people who have contributed to this issue by helping us with comments, advice or suggestions, we would like to thank especially Nancy Bedford, Edward Farrugia, Stephanie Feder, Rosino Gibellini, Heike Harbecke, Marcia Hermansen, Maureen Junker-Kenny, Kyung-Sook Lee, Harry McSorley, Enzo Pace, Tracy Pintchman, Norbert Reck, Luiz Susin, Christoph Theobald and Annette Wilke. Our thanks for a lot of work on the bibliography at the end of this issue go to Franziska Birke, Heike Harbecke and Jesse Perillo.

Concilium Subscription Information

February   2007/1: *Theological and Religious Pluralism*

April   2007/2: *The Land*

June   2007/3: *Aids*

October   2007/4: *Christianity and Democracy*

December   2007/5: *Ages of Life and Christian Experiences*

New subscribers: to receive *Concilium 2007* (five issues) anywhere in the world, please copy this form, complete it in block capitals and send it with your payment to the address below.

- -

Please enter my subscription for *Concilium 2007*

Individuals

____ £40.00 UK
____ $110.00 North America/Rest of World
____ €99.00 Europe

Institutions

____ £55.00 UK
____ $140 North America/Rest of World
____ €125.00. Europe

Postage included – airmail for overseas subscribers

Payment Details:

Payment must accompany all orders and can be made by cheque or credit card

I enclose a cheque for £/$/€ _____ Payable to SCM-Canterbury Press Ltd

Please charge my Visa/MasterCard (Delete as appropriate) for £/$/€ _____

Credit card number ....

Expiry date ....

Signature of cardholder ....

Name on card ....

Telephone .... E-mail ....

Send your order to *Concilium*, SCM-Canterbury Press Ltd
9–17 St Albans Place, London N1 ONX, UK
Tel +44 (0)20 7359 8033 Fax +44 (0)20 7359 0049
E-Mail: office@scm-canterburypress.co.uk

Customer service information:
All orders must be prepaid. Subscriptions are entered on an annual basis (i.e. January to December). No refunds on subscriptions will be made after the first issue of the Journal has been despatched. If you have any queries or require information about other payment methods, please contact our Customer Services department.